# Run It like a
# Business

Top Financial
Planners Weigh
In on Practice
Management

## Richard J. Koreto

**Dearborn™**
Trade Publishing
A **Kaplan Professional** Company

This publication is designed to provide accurate and authoritative information in regard to the subject matter covered. It is sold with the understanding that the publisher is not engaged in rendering legal, accounting, or other professional service. If legal advice or other expert assistance is required, the services of a competent professional should be sought.

Vice President and Publisher: Cynthia A. Zigmund
Acquisitions Editor: Mary B. Good
Senior Project Editor: Trey Thoelcke
Interior Design: Lucy Jenkins
Cover Design: Scott Rattray, Rattray Design
Typesetting: the dotted i

Published by Dearborn Trade Publishing
A Kaplan Professional Company

Printed in the United States of America

04 05 06   10 9 8 7 6 5 4 3 2 1

**Library of Congress Cataloging-in-Publication Data**

Koreto, Richard J.
    Run it like a business : top financial planners weigh in on practice management / Richard J. Koreto.
        p.      cm.
    ISBN 0-7931-8338-3
    1. Financial planners.    2. Small business—Management.    I. Title.
HG179.5.K67 2004
332.024—dc22

                                        2003023852

Dearborn Trade Publishing books are available at special quantity discounts to use for sales promotions, employee premiums, or educational purposes. Please contact our special sales department, to order or for more information, at trade@dearborn.com or 800-245-2665, or write to Dearborn Financial Publishing, 30 South Wacker Drive, Suite 2500, Chicago, IL 60606-7481.

For Elizabeth, without whom there would be no book, no anything.

# Contents

**C**ongratulations! You deserve it because you have just done something to improve your life. Simply by purchasing this book, you have taken one of the most positive steps you can towards increasing your income and serving your clients. As executive editor of *Financial Planning* magazine, Richard Koreto is continually in contact with the most successful financial advisors in the nation and, over the years, has developed a keen understanding of what it takes to build a financial planning practice business that can outlive you.

In *Run It like a Business: Top Financial Planners Weigh In on Practice Management,* Richard presents the best ideas of the best in the business. There is something in this book for every advisor who wants to take control of his or her life and business. You'll probably be flooded with great ideas after reading this, but if you take only one jewel out this, it could change your life forever. Imagine the time you would need to go through all the material that Richard did, talk to all the advisors he did, and boil it all down to what would work best for you. As I read through the text, I found myself looking for that one magic bullet or common thread that would be the key to success for financial advisors. As I was devouring all the success stories (another reason why you'll love this book), I realized what the message was. There is no magic bullet, or if there is one, it is unique for each advisor. As you read, you'll find yourself saying something like, "I can do that," or, "That would be perfect for me," or, "What a great idea." You might even say, "That may work for another advisor, but it's just not my style," and that insight is worthwhile too. These interviews will get you motivated.

They'll start you thinking about how you can adapt these ideas and strategies to your particular business model and clientele.

This book will help you find the magic bullet that works for you. It probably took an average of 20 years for each of the successful financial advisors featured here to find their magic bullets, but thanks to Richard, you don't have to wait a fraction of that time. You may even want to jump right into a certain section, which is easy to do, and come up with a great idea within minutes of opening the book. The book is set up so you can dig in anywhere you like. Another great feature is that Richard not only asks the advisors about what worked but also highlights failures, so that you don't have to waste time and money going down a dead end. You are also likely to pick up valuable business-building ideas from what didn't work.

The bottom line is that this book will change your life, opening you up to treating your practice like a business and setting it up in a way that works best for you, your staff, and, of course, your valued clients. It's time to dig in and start building a financial planning business that will take care of you and your family for the rest of your lives. That's the perfect financial plan. Good Luck!

—Ed Slott

I got the idea for this book—along with a rap across my knuckles and an earful of obscenities—about ten years ago. I was covering the accounting profession for a trade journal. My editor had told me to interview a CPA who had a small but extremely successful accounting practice. Working with both his state CPA society and the American Institute of CPAs, he put together some great programs to help small accounting firms better manage their practices and effectively deliver accounting, tax, and financial planning services. His goal, he told me, was to get CPAs to think like *businesspeople*—an alien concept for a group that liked to think of themselves as professionals, on an equal footing with physicians and lawyers.

So I wrote the story, but my editor deleted the quotes about "thinking like businesspeople," saying she was not about to face the rage of thousands of readers who found themselves demoted from lofty professionals to mere businesspeople.

When the article appeared, the furious subject of my story called, wanting to know why I hadn't included his comments on thinking like a *businessperson*. I told him why. "You missed the whole point!" He punctuated his opinions with some colorful language and hung up on me.

I danced around this issue for the next decade—not just for accountants but for a range of financial professionals, especially financial planners. As a group, they have fought a good fight, a successful fight, to be seen as true advisors, true professionals, not product pushers. The *professional* label was especially important to them.

Yet . . . like accountants, doctors, and lawyers, they were running a business. No professional seems to want to admit that, but, in fact, they are running a business, and there's nothing shameful about it. Quite the opposite. I began to notice that some of the most effective financial planners, the ones who had full rosters of satisfied clients, were also exceptionally good at managing their financial planning businesses. It seemed that client care, ethical behavior, portfolio management skills, and basic financial planning know-how were not divorced from plain old capitalistic business management. Rather, they were an integral part of it.

In fact, when I tried to find a point of similarity among the best planners I knew—whether they handled just a dozen multi-millionaires or hundreds of middle-income families—I discovered they were all good businesspeople. Their effective business skills allowed them to spend more of their firms' time on actual planning tasks.

I called them up and asked them to share their practice management insights—their tips, guidance, and even mistakes. I began collecting the practice management wisdom of the most successful planners, adding as well what I observed from the hundreds of interviews, seminars, and conferences I attended over the years.

I thought that, in the end, I'd come up with a lot of agreement—one right way to set up an office, one right computer to buy, one kind of staffing solution. I could thus come up with the ultimate best practices.

But it was not that simple. As I spoke to the experts and reviewed past articles I had written, I realized there were dozens of solutions, dozens of effective ways of running a practice. True success for the top planners was finding a path that fit their specific goals, desires, and personalities. So as you read through this book, you will rarely find one correct way of doing anything. Rather, you will find one or more planners like you, who have found solutions you can use and adapt to your practice. This book will not help you find *the* right way, but *your* right way.

For example, you'll meet planners who practice alone, or maybe just with one assistant, not because this is all they are capable of, but because that's how they choose to run their practice. It's what makes sense to them professionally and personally. You'll meet others who have many employees and enjoy running a larger business. Some work with clients with millions to invest, others with just thousands—again, not because they failed to get the high-net-worth clients, but because they wanted to work with middle-income clients.

Each model is different, but each is the creation of a planner who knew the practice needed to be run like a business, and that's what all the experts in this book have in common. They all knew that you could be the best advisor in the world, but when you sit behind a desk, your practice will go nowhere if you aren't a good businessperson, too.

Of course, there was no way I could distill the complete thoughts of even one successful planner or expert, let alone the 20 or so I interviewed for this book. As you grow, and depending how you grow, you will need to read other books, too, so I have listed some of them in the Resources. I designed this book to get you started, so it is *not* the last word on practice management. On the contrary, it is the *first* word on practice management.

If you run your practice like a business, you'll have happy clients, a happy staff, and a happy professional life. You will have the best of both worlds—as a successful professional and a successful businessperson.

## HOW TO USE THIS BOOK

If you're just starting out, read it from cover to cover. Although each chapter is self-contained, I followed a rough chronological order for setting up a practice: you can't have a marketing plan until you have a computer, and you can't have a computer until you have an office to put it in, for example. Then, you can use the book as a reference as you continue to run your practice.

If you're at least somewhat established, read what works for you. If you're happy with your office, skip that chapter. If you're the kind of person who relaxes in the evening with *PC Magazine,* you may not need the tech chapter.

At the end, I included some appendices—helpful books, Web sites, technology companies. Everyone will find these useful.

Finally, everyone should also read the list of experts in the Introduction. Their full biographies are there in alphabetical order. You can see why I chose to quote them in the book. If you have any questions for them after reading this book and see one of them at a conference, introduce yourself. Not only do all these experts know how to run their practice like a business, they also all enjoy meeting colleagues, discussing the profession, and sharing their thoughts. Perhaps that's one of the reasons they're so successful.

**I**t was astonishing at first to re-alize—with growing panic—how many people I would rely on to write this book, and, as the project proceeded, to realize—with growing relief—how forthcoming everyone was.

First, I'd like to thank the experts I interviewed for the book: Morris Armstrong, Bill Bachrach, John Bowen, Mark Calhoun, Ric Edelman, Sheryl Garrett, Andy Gluck, David Grau, Nancy Langdon Jones, Alan Kahn, Deena Katz, Sharon Kayfetz, Amy Leavitt, Ross Levin, Michael Lovas, Dan Moisand, John Olsen, François Quinson, Jeffrey Rattiner, Don Schreiber, Ed Slott, Louis Stanasolovich, and Mark Tibergien. All of these busy people gave a lot of their time. In addition, Tibergien pulled together some of Moss Adams's invaluable data for me to republish, and Grau kindly granted me permission to use several excellent charts from FP Transitions's most recent Practice Transitions Report.

Not one person I approached for an interview turned me down. In fact, they all got back to me in a couple of days, some-times a couple of hours, after I requested an interview. The cyn-ical might say that they helped me because of the marketing advantage they might reap from getting their name in this book. But, considering how successful they are already, this book is hardly likely to give them a major push. In fact, one person, set-ting himself up as a spokesperson for all of them, said, "Richard, we're all cooperating because we know you're going to make us look good." Flattering, but as an explanation, it doesn't fly.

I think they all helped because of a knee-jerk reaction. They are successful because they like helping other people, and when I asked for help, an automatic response kicked in. That reac-tion is probably worth more than any advice I can give.

I'd like to thank Larry Chambers for his help in identifying some big players in this field and for letting me sit in on one of his presentations, which was about as much fun as I've ever had in a financial planning conference.

Although I drew on the wisdom of the people I interviewed, I also relied on many people over the years whose generosity gave me the background and knowledge to write this book. The unfailingly helpful staff at the FPA, NAPFA, and AICPA have put me in touch with scores of practitioners over the years and have always made me welcome at their conferences. I'm grateful to Lois Whitehead at the New York State Society of CPAs, who has invited me to so many of the Society's events and has sent so many great contacts my way.

I'd like to thank my colleagues at Thomson Media, past and present. They have made working on *Financial Planning* magazine and Financial-Planning.com not only professionally satisfying but a pleasure. My former colleagues at the *Journal of Accountancy* bear some responsibility for whatever is good in this book, for teaching me how to write about practice management in financial services.

Mary B. Good, my editor at Dearborn, has been a continual source of enthusiasm since she first considered my book idea and was enormously helpful when I was assembling my proposal. Project editor Trey Thoelcke improved the book greatly with his suggestions. My thanks to both of them and all the other helpful people at Dearborn.

On the home front, thanks to my parents, Paul and Vivienne Koreto, who supported every writing initiative I've ever had. My terrific daughters, Katie and Sophie, have been absolutely wonderful about not bothering Daddy while he was writing his book. Finally, and most importantly, thanks to my wife, Liz, for all her patience, love, and practical help while I spent long evenings and weekends locked in the office.

However, despite the large network I called on to help me, any shortcomings are mine entirely.

# SAGE ADVICE

The first key feature of this book is the advice and commentary of distinguished and articulate planners and other authorities in the financial universe. You may want to know why, of the thousands of financial planners out there, you should you accept the advice of the ones in this book. The profiles below should make it clear why these are the people to listen to. Some of them have written books—which I have listed and heartily recommend.

Morris Armstrong, CFP, ChFC, CDP, of Armstrong Financial Strategies in New Milford, Connecticut <www.armstrong-financial.com>, has helped me out with scores of stories over the years. A 30-year veteran of the financial services industry, he has managed portfolios of currencies and bonds for a number of leading financial institutions, among them the Bank of America, Bank of New York, and ABN-Amro. He has been quoted in major publications on a variety of planning and divorce issues.

Bill Bachrach, CSP, of Bachrach and Associates, Inc., in San Diego <www.bachrachvbs.com>, came to my attention when he was selected as a "Mover & Shaker" by *Financial Planning* magazine readers. I interviewed him for the magazine and described him as a well-regarded sales authority who doesn't much like salesmanship. A dynamic and in-demand speaker, he has been a frequent guest at the Million Dollar Round Table, the Financial Planning Association Success Form, and the MDRT Top of the Table. He has written or cowritten several excellent books, including *Values-Based Selling, It's All about Them: How Trusted Advisors Listen for Success, High-Trust Leadership,* and *Values-Based Financial Planning* (for consumers).

John Bowen, of CEG Worldwide in San Martin, California <www.cegworldwide.com>, is the person I call whenever I need advice about the industry's direction. He always knows what's going on. Bowen is a leading authority on the investment advisory business, and his firm is an unparalleled resource for advice and research for investment advisors. He previously was CEO of Reinhardt Werba Bowen Advisory Services, where he managed over $1.6 billion in assets under management, and president and CEO of Assante Capital Management. He is a much-read columnist at *Financial Planning*. His books include *The Prudent Investor's Guide to Beating the Market, The Prudent Investor's Guide to Beating Wall Street at Its Own Game,* and *Creating Equity: How to Build a Hugely Successful Asset Management Business.*

Mark Calhoun, of Etelligent Consulting in Overland Park, Kansas <www.etelligentconsulting.com>, is one of those rare people who know about technology *and* finance. This is why I've found it almost impossible to do a technology story without calling him or one of the other people at Etelligent. Calhoun is Series 65 registered as well as a Microsoft Certified Systems Engineer. He is active as a financial planner and has over a decade of experience in the technology industry as a consultant and consulting director for Fortune 500 and Fortune 1000 clients.

Ric Edelman, CFS, RFC, CMFC, CRC, QFP, of Edelman Financial Services, Inc., in Fairfax, Virginia <www.ricedelman .com>, is nationally known as a dynamic speaker, and he's equally exciting in face-to-face interviews. A former journalist, he has built his practice into one of the largest and most successful financial planning firms in the country. He is an award-winning radio talk-show host, TV host, and columnist. Royal Alliance, his broker-dealer, has honored him three times. He has written five books: *Ordinary People, Extraordinary Wealth; The New Rules of Money; The Truth about Money; Discover the Wealth within You;* and *What You Need to Do Now.* They have collectively sold more than 1 million copies.

Sheryl Garrett, CFP, of The Garrett Planning Network, Inc. in Shawnee, Kansas <GarrettPlanningNetwork.com>, a *Financial Planning* "Mover & Shaker," is one of the true innovators of the profession. She first created a highly successful, fee-only firm aimed at middle-income and "validator" clients, then followed up by extending her model into a rapidly growing network of planners. Her success has made her one of the most widely quoted planners in the media today. She has written *Garrett's Guide to Financial Planning—How to Capture the Middle Market and Increase Your Profits,* and, with other network members, *Just Give Me the Answer$: Expert Advisors Address Your Most Pressing Financial Questions.*

Andy Gluck, of AdvisorProducts, Inc., in Westbury, New York <www.advisorproducts.com>, wears multiple hats as the irrepressible columnist for *Investment Advisor* magazine and as a successful entrepreneur who creates Web sites, brochures, and newsletters for advisors. Earlier he had been a senior writer at *Worth* magazine and a reporter at *The Daily News* of New York, where he covered Wall Street and wrote a weekly investment column. His continual journalistic investigations into the state of the profession ensure that he creates up-to-date products for advisors.

David Grau, of FP Transitions in Portland, Oregon <www.FPTransitions.com>, has been at the forefront of his firm's pioneering a whole new line of work—brokering the buying and selling of financial planning practices. Grau is president of the parent firm, Business Transitions, a leading facilitator of buying and selling advisory, accounting, and insurance practices on its Web sites: FPTransitions.com, CPAtransitions.com, and Insurancetransitions.com. Along the way, Grau and his associates learned a great deal about who buys practices and why. No reporter can do a story about the buying, selling, and evaluation of practices without talking with Grau.

Nancy Langdon Jones, CFP, of NLJones, Inc., in Upland, California <www.nljones.com>, doesn't have an area in which she stands out. She has *many* areas. While running a successful, fee-only practice out of her home, she is also deeply involved in the growth of the profession. She's been a leader in creating an internship program for would-be planners, an activist moderator in the Financial-Planning.com discussion boards, a speaker, and a member of many professional organizations. Jones managed to create a series of options within her small practice to serve many clients and found ways to reach out despite operating out of a small office. She's a *Financial Planning* "Mover & Shaker" and one of the shrewdest practice management experts working today. Her book, *So You Want to Be a Financial Planner,* is a must-read for any new planner.

Alan Kahn, CPA, CLU, ChFC, of the AJK Financial Group in Syosset, New York <www.ajkfinancialgroup.com>, is a mainstay of the New York State Society of CPAs, where he has showed himself to be both a PR whiz and a leading expert on estate planning and other financial issues. He is widely quoted in the press and appears regularly on television—and has adorned the cover of *Financial Planning* magazine.

Deena Katz, of Evensky, Brown & Katz in Coral Gables, Florida <www.evensky.com>, has, along with her partner (and husband) Harold Evensky, helped spawn an unwritten rule among financial journalists: you can't write a major article without quoting someone from this firm. Probably no one knows more about practice management than Deena Katz, and probably no one knows more about investing than Evensky. The two of them were *Financial Planning* "Movers & Shakers," and Katz has spoken nationally at many conferences and has been quoted in more media than I can list. She was the first woman director of a United States Rotary Club. Her books, *Deena Katz on Practice Management* and *Deena Katz's Tools & Templates for Your Practice,* should be on every planner's bookshelf.

Sharon Kayfetz, CFP, in California <www.paperlessoffice .org> has probably pushed the technology envelope further than any other planner. She managed to achieve a completely paperless office, enabling a whole new practice model, and has lectured widely on this model. She has had a consulting practice on paperless techniques since 1998.

Kayfetz (also known by her pen names Sharon Sinpapel and Sharon A.C. Chatten) is the author of *The Virtual Office for the Visionary Enterprise.*

Amy Leavitt, CFP, of Leavitt Associates in Quechee, Vermont, is one of those planners who saw a new way to handle her practice and ran with it. She was one of the first to realize that the investment product is the commodity and the planner's advice is what you sell. She molded her practice around this concept and became so successful, she found herself lecturing to other planners in sellout seminars. She is one of the best speakers on the conference circuit.

Ross Levin, CFP, of Accredited Investors in Edina, Minnesota <www.accredited.com>, is a true investing innovator and actually created an investing scoring system, which he described in his book, *The Wealth Management Index: The Financial Advisor's System for Assessing & Managing Your Client's Plans & Goals.* Exceptionally articulate, he has been quoted in virtually every major financial publication and has been seen on *Oprah* and *CBS This Morning.* He's a past chairman of the International Association for Financial Planning, predecessor to the FPA, and was a *Financial Planning* "Mover & Shaker."

Michael Lovas, of AboutPeople, in Dallas, Texas <www .aboutpeople.com>, first came to my attention when I heard him speak. I knew I had to get him to write an article for *Financial Planning,* and then I knew I had to interview him for this book. With a degree in Human Relations in Business, he is also a clinical hypnotherapist, a Master Practitioner of Neurolinguistic Programming, and a language and behavior specialist. A terrific speaker, he has an astonishing way of looking at one-on-one interactions, allowing you to see how you truly work with your clients. He is the author of three books: *Beyond Wave Marketing: How to Add Credibility to Your Relationship Marketing Program, Face Values: How to Read People and Motivate Them in 3*

*Minutes!*, and *The Emotional Connection: How to Build a Powerful Bond with Your Clients.*

Dan Moisand, CFP, of Spraker, Fitzgerald, Tamayo & Moisand in Melbourne, Florida <www.sprakerfitzgerald.com>, came to everyone's attention when he published an incisive, award-winning paper on how he searched for a firm to merge his solo practice with. He gave voice to a lot of other planners struggling with the same issue. However, this *Financial Planning* "Mover & Shaker" has had other distinguished achievements as well. He is on the National Board of Directors of the FPA, he was chairman of the FPA National Professional Issues Subcommittee, and he spent three years on the CFP Board of Practice Standards.

John Olsen, CLU, ChFC, of the Olsen Financial Group in Kirkwood, Missouri <www.olsenfinancialgroup.com>, is one of the most tech-savvy planners in the business and is an invaluable resource as moderator of the Financial.Planning.com software discussion room. He's made his tech skills serve him in setting up and running a successful, multifaceted practice out of his home. Olsen has produced the first of a series of continuing education CDs, the first one being *Annuities: Structure, Cost, and Benefits.*

François L. Quinson has consulted extensively on organizational, performance and compensation issues with senior management of corporations of all sizes from large multinationals operating around the globe to organizations with a regional or even local focus, in the industrial, financial, and service sectors. After a 25-year consulting career with a number of firms, including the Hay Group and Mercer, he is now an independent consultant to a wide variety of organizations in the United States and abroad with primary emphasis on strategic organization design; planning for management selection, development, and continuity; performance management and contracts; and compensation strategies. Over the years he has conducted seminars on these topics in North and South America, Europe, Africa, and Asia.

Jeffrey Rattiner, CPA, CFP, RFC, of JR Financial Group in Englewood, Colorado <www.jrfinancialgroup.com>, is the profession's Renaissance man. He runs a financial planning firm, an investment advisory firm, and a tax preparation firm. With a local college, he runs his unique Fast Track training program for those who want to be CFPs—worth a look by anyone who does not yet have this designation. A columnist for *Financial Planning*, he also has found the time to write several books, including *Rattiner's Financial Planner's Bible, Getting Started as a Financial Planner, Adding Personal Financial Planning to Your Practice*, and *The Practitioner's Guide to Personal Financial Planning*. Earlier in his career, he worked for the CFP Board, the Institute of CFPs, and the American Institute of CPAs.

Don Schreiber, Jr., CFP, CEO of Wealth Builders, Inc., in Little Silver, New Jersey <www.wbadvisory.com>, has shown himself an exceptional leader in recruiting and training an effective and loyal staff, especially in a field where so many struggle with human resource issues. In fact, on his Web site he notes: "We believe in teamwork and are committed to each other. We need to attract and retain talented people. We run our business, we do not let our business run us." He has been quoted and profiled in leading publications and is the author of *Building a World Class Financial Services Business*.

Ed Slott, CPA, of E. Slott & Company in Rockville Centre, New York <www.irahelp.com>, is probably the nation's leading IRA expert, but it's his boundless enthusiasm that has made him such an extraordinary success. He is one of the most indemand—and entertaining—financial speakers in the country, and it's difficult to find a business publication in which he has *not* been quoted or a business TV show in which he has *not* appeared. A regular contributor to *Financial Planning*, he won an award from the CFP Board for a past article. His recent book, *The Retirement Savings Time Bomb and How to Defuse It*, should be required reading for all planners and their clients.

Louis Stanasolovich, CFP, of Legend Financial Advisors in Pittsburgh, Pennsylvania <www.legend-financial.com>, is one of the profession's deep thinkers and has made his mark in more than one area. In practice management, his pioneering use of an open-book management office, matched with effective use of interns, has made his firm one of the best run anywhere. His expertise in portfolio management has not only earned him the gratitude of his clients but led him to positions on the TIAA-CREF Institute's advisory board and the TD Waterhouse Advisory Council. He has also been involved in a variety of professional organizations and has been quoted in dozens of publications.

Mark Tibergien, of Moss Adams Advisory Services, in Seattle, Washington <www.mossadams.com>, became one of the top authorities on what works in financial planning and what doesn't by creating his invaluable benchmarking studies for the profession. His speaking sessions at top conferences are must-attend events for any planner interested in where the profession is going—and what your role in the future can or should be. He was recently named a *Financial Planning* "Mover & Shaker."

## ADVICE IN ACTION

The second key feature of this book consists of the case studies. These fictional stories illustrate how planners might apply the lessons learned in each chapter. Although these have been simplified for illustrative purposes, they present true problems planners may face. I have provided at least one solution, and sometimes more, based on the advice the industry experts have given. After reading the book and looking at your own experience, you may think of still more—and I hope you do, because that is how you will grow and improve as a professional.

Of course, nothing in these case studies—indeed, in this book—is meant to supersede dictates from regulatory bodies or advice from compliance experts at a broker-dealer, custodian, or consulting firm. But the case studies will show you succinctly how you might apply the advice.

# 1

# A PLACE TO HANG
# YOUR HAT

**O**ne of my first job interviews
when I got out of college was at an elegant midtown New York
office. The reception area failed to impress, however, being
adorned by some straggly, tree-like plants and lots of rocks. I
think the designer was trying to achieve the sophisticated sim-
plicity of a Japanese rock garden and had failed miserably.

"Do you like our office design?" asked the receptionist
brightly. "It was designed by the CEO's wife."

God bless her. She had probably saved dozens of suppliers,
clients, and job applicants from embarrassing themselves with
comments on the odd and depressing décor. She understood,
if her boss did not, that an office's style and location says something about the business—and what theirs said wasn't good.

The same is true for your business. Once upon a time, a
successful business, certainly a financial business, meant a well-
respected address and solid wood furniture. Eventually, lots of
chrome and glass could do the same trick. But today—bad rock

gardens aside—there are many ways to set up an office and establish a professional look.

Of course, the big decision isn't wood versus chrome. It's home versus outside office. It's true that working out of your home—no matter how big and gracious your home was—used to be an absolute no-no. What was wrong with you that you couldn't afford an office? That attitude has changed, and there's a lot to be said, particularly when you're starting out, for working out of your home.

Even when you're not starting out. Some planners have had a long and successful practice working out of their homes, even though they are well able to afford an outside office. In parsimonious times, some clients may take satisfaction in knowing that their fees are not going into a lot of overhead.

## HOME IS WHERE THE OFFICE IS

Take Nancy Langdon Jones. She fully expected to work in an office when she set up her practice, back in the 1980s. She started out, like many new businesses, in rented space in an executive suite. These are basically offices-in-a-box. If you search online for "executive suites," you'll find them in the business districts of big and even not-so-big cities all over the country. No worry, no mess: pay a monthly rent/fee for as much office space as you need, including conference rooms. You usually get to share a receptionist and other office support. During business hours, an actual person, not voice mail, answers your phone. This arrangement can be a great, if sometimes pricey, way to start out, if there's one in your location.

Jones started at one happily, then decided to switch to a new office suite complex. "They came over soliciting tenants for the new complex, and I was going to share a suite with an attorney and a CPA. I put my furniture in storage, my husband and I went on vacation, and we expected to come back and move in. But they didn't finish the complex. Still, I needed a place to work, so I cleared off the dining room table, got some furniture out of storage, and started seeing clients temporarily at home." She never thought it would work for more than a brief period. "So many distractions—we had dogs, there was TV, always dishes and laundry and stuff to do." But she was pleasantly surprised: "I found that clients just opened up so much more in a home environment. We were so relaxed. We're doing financial planning, and it's important for clients to open up. Before long I realized that I should have been working at home all along."

As an added bonus, there was the tax savings on her house. Her children disappeared to college, and her office expanded into their bedrooms. "Now I have the original office, a conference room, storage room, private office—all former bedrooms—and then I also write off part of the living area. It's fixed up like a reception area, and that's all it's used for." When she needs a larger conference room, she can still rent an executive suite by the day at an affordable price.

Just two warnings. You do need a house that can accommodate this. Jones says, "In our home, you can come in the front door and walk right down the hall to my offices, without going anywhere else or disturbing other activities that may be going on." Also, you have to remember that when you work at home, you never leave. "You have to draw a line between work and home, period," she says—and then laughs. "But I can't do it!" Although she has separate phone lines for home and office, she admits she can't resist a ringing phone, even in the evening. "My clients know I'm here, but you know what? I'm glad I'm here for them."

John Bowen, perhaps the leading consultant to the profession, is even more blunt about the advantages of working at home. "You just don't need a decadent office," he says. "Have it in your home. And keep it small." Even 1,000–1,500 square feet will do for a small or beginning practice.

Looked at another way, "How real does this office have to be?" asks Bowen, who makes his business work virtually, as noted in the technology chapter. Bowen meets his clients in his pool house office, and considering he sends out six-figure bills, he's hardly a struggling beginner. "It's the type of positioning I chose to do for my business. I certainly could afford to have a really nice office downtown. But I'm in shorts and Top-Siders all day—it's not a bad lifestyle."

No beginner, either, is Morris Armstrong, and he works out of his home. In all his years of practice, he's only found one client who was uncomfortable with the arrangement. Like many planners I've spoken with, he sometimes takes his office on the road, in fact, working in his clients' homes and offices. "It can be more convenient for them. When you meet a client at their home or office, everything is available. There's no, 'Oh, I forgot that statement, I forgot that tax document.'" He's considering establishing a small satellite office in another Connecticut town, which would be affordable because his main office would remain in his home.

Sharon Kayfetz, who has maintained a large practice as an independent rep, has been able to operate with an office-on-the-road by securely storing client records on her laptop and working at clients' homes. This visiting model works for a variety of practices and clients. I know a Chicago-area accountant, for example, who does tax returns for very wealthy clients. He makes appointments to deliver the returns personally at clients' homes, letting them review the returns and ask him questions right then and there. His clients, he says, love the personal attention.

Ultimately, such visiting means that you can reduce office size and be more flexible about location, because the office is less likely to be a central point for clients. Visiting also makes a home office more possible.

# KEEPING THE OFFICE AT THE OFFICE

But a home office isn't going to work for everyone. Your house may not have an appropriate layout or may simply be too small. Perhaps it may be too far from the beaten path, making it difficult for most of your clients to visit, or it might be full of young children. Also, your clients may be rather traditional and don't want their business advisors in their homes.

The home office just may not be the image you want to project.

That's certainly what Amy Leavitt felt. Today, in addition to being a successful planner, she also is a nationally known speaker. But even from the beginning, she had an office. "From the very beginning, even before I could afford it, I wanted to have a professional image and have an office. I thought that, once you're successful, you can end up having an office in your home, but for building a business, it didn't have the right image."

However, Leavitt practices in rural Vermont, near the New Hampshire border, in a town that has fewer residents than many planners have clients. It doesn't have a lot of executive suites or many office buildings. "We didn't have much choice about spaces." She had to be creative. Her first office was in an old bank building, where the top floors had been partitioned into offices. Next, an old library rented out space. Eventually, she bought her own building, where she practices today, on Main Street, Quechee, Vermont. An office building purchase is generally financially impossible in New York or Chicago business districts but remains a nice option in smaller locales.

Dan Moisand tried just about every option, however, and found pluses and minuses all around. While he was weighing the advantages of different funds and the impact of new tax regulations, he also felt it was important to reflect on driving directions and greedy forest creatures.

"When my original partner and I left American Express, our offices were in an eight-story building in a congested, high-traffic area. Many of our clients found it difficult to access the parking lot—we saw accidents about twice a week. We knew we wanted something a little more user-friendly."

They found a suite in a building on a golf course. "It looked a lot like a house, and it was divided into three suites. You could pull up to the curb, walk 15 feet and go in the front door." Nice? To a point. "When you have a small suite like we did, even though there's a landlord to take care of building and grounds, you found yourself doing housekeeping. If you pulled up to your office and found a raccoon had gotten into the trash in the night, you had to clean it up."

When the partnership dissolved, Moisand decided to make things easy and moved into an executive suite. "Clerical help, office support, and a human to answer the phone during business hours—clients love that. The suite is in an easy-to-find building with plenty of parking access. There's even a steak house downstairs for entertaining." Moisand merged his practice with a firm in a nearby town recently, but he's so happy with his suite, he's staying put.

## GETTING BIGGER

As we'll see in future chapters, some planners, no matter where they work, will always have a small office. This is *not* because they fail to thrive but because that's the way they want to practice. However, if you grow your practice to the point where it includes other planners and extensive support staff, you're going to have to find an office. If you plan to continue to grow, you'll have to allow for expansion. (If you and your spouse plan on children, you probably wouldn't buy a studio apartment.)

Sheryl Garrett, with her Midwest practice, was disappointed in her search for a home office but came to see this as a blessing in disguise. Not only did her practice take off in a big way, but she became the creator and manager of a network of planners.

When she created her current practice about six years ago, she was looking to make a lot of changes in the services she offered and in the way she offered them. "I was trying to find a way to keep costs down. I wanted to simplify things and reduce the headaches that came with staff and overhead and all." She shopped around for a commercial property that also had a residential apartment but found nothing she liked. So she purchased an office condominium and kept her house. Like Amy Leavitt, she was in a market where business properties were affordable even if you weren't Donald Trump.

"I eventually outgrew that, and because of the network, with a need for training in-house, another investor and I bought a building about three years ago. In our market, in our town, it's a lot cheaper than renting."

Both Leavitt and Garrett ended up just fine, but moving isn't fun, and there's the expense of new business cards and new stationery. Also, it's expensive to buy or rent space you don't need yet, even if you're confident you'll grow into it.

Ross Levin worked out a nice compromise by taking space in a building large enough to accommodate a larger practice later. He and his partner started with 3,000 square feet, enough room for the two of them plus a secretary. Gradually, they added suites within the building. "Now we have 5,000 square feet." It's not contiguous within the building—the new half is across the hall—but at least a major move wasn't necessary. He also adjusted his lease to allow himself an out to expand further. He, too, is considering a building purchase, so his current lease is for three years with a three-year renewal option. Levin is also willing to take a gamble on growth. "Maybe we could find 10,000–15,000 square feet, clearly more than we need right now."

Lou Stanasolovich, in an urban area, got sophisticated in how he managed his office and went toe-to-toe with his landlord. "When we started out, it was basically a matter of what we could afford—and what the landlord would allow us to do. With one building we wanted, they wanted us to put up all the costs of the improvement and a letter of credit. This would mean not necessarily borrowing money, but tapping our line of credit to secure that letter of credit. So we didn't do that and instead went to a landlord that was friendly. We found one who didn't even require a deposit."

Surely you've heard of bond ladders? Stanasolovich used a rent ladder. "We learned to structure our leases in a step-rated fashion. We basically pay $100,000 a year in rent. After the first year, we paid about $66,000, which was a big jump from the initial $32,000. We grew into the rent." They paid more than the going rate in later years, but this allowed the firm to grow into its expenses as the revenue grew.

That was a good start, but Stanasolovich became a victim of his own success. "Even so, we're now maxed out in space and only halfway through a six-year lease." Still, he has a novel solution to maximizing space. He says with a laugh: "I keep threatening my staff that we're going to three eight-hour shifts."

## COMPLETELY VIRTUAL

Conventional wisdom holds that a home office is only for very small outfits—planners working by themselves or maybe with one assistant. But advances in technology, and accompanying psychological adjustments, have made it possible to get more employees *and* work at home. That is, you work at your home, while your employees work at theirs.

It's possible, and it's already been done. David Drucker and Joel Bruckenstein have addressed this in their excellent book, *Virtual-Office Tools for a High-Margin Practice.* One of their case studies is Carolyn Sechler, a CPA in Phoenix, who started this type of office years ago. She employs a mix of regular staff and independent contractors and maintains no true central office.

Other planners have done this to a certain extent as well. John Bowen's assistant lives on the other side of the country. Nancy Langdon Jones refers to Michael Ling, who provides investment advice, as a member of her team—but he lives in Idaho, while her office is in California. Dan Moisand merged his practice with a larger firm but has kept his individual office. You could argue Ed Slott works this way; on the road so often with his speaking engagements, he has to rely on his staff to run the firm without his frequent physical presence.

However, growing a completely decentralized practice with multiple employees and team members presents some unique advantages and problems. On the plus side are the cost savings from not renting an office and a happy workforce that can avoid commuting. You never have a staff member who has to leave early because children are coming home from school or the plumber is expected to show up. There is a technological hurdle, but if you're willing to spend the money upfront, a technology consulting firm (see the Tech chapter) can wire everyone together from their homes.

The main drawback may be psychological. Are you comfortable not seeing members of your staff every day? Is this how you want to supervise staff? (See the Human Resources chapter for more on supervision.) You need a self-motivated group of people who are also comfortable with technology. One company started allowing, even encouraging, employees in a certain department to work at home, as a pilot project. The employees loved it, and the company noted no decline in productivity. But the administrative assistant for the team, although responsible and self-motivated, never felt comfortable with the technology and became increasingly unhappy at the "disconnection." Eventually, the company had to find her an equivalent position in another department and hired a new employee for the off-site group.

You also need clients who are comfortable with this model. It's one thing to tell a client you have an office in your home and another to tell him his accounts will be shared in homes all across town. The client has to feel there will be no loss of privacy and control; not every client will be happy about this.

If you are comfortable with using technology to stay in touch and this sounds like an exciting idea, read Drucker and Bruckenstein's book and consider this as a model. However, keep in mind that you don't have to start virtually—a traditional firm can migrate to a virtual one over time. And don't lose the personal touch with clients or employees. Get together with staff as time allows. Back in 1998, I interviewed the partners at K2 Enterprises, a financial-oriented training and consulting firm whose far-flung members used sophisticated techniques to keep in touch while on the road. Still, one of the partners told me, "We try very hard to meet face-to-face once a month. Nothing is the same as face-to-face."

## TAKE IT SLOWLY

Are you more confused about offices now than when you started reading this? That's okay—a normal reaction. Deena Katz, who probably knows more about running a successful practice than anyone, advises being flexible and taking it slowly.

"I started out like everybody else—just me! You can do what I did and find a related firm—in my case, a real estate management company—that had some extra space. I didn't have to fork over a lot of money for the space right away, until I saw what kind of business I was going to get and how it was going to work out." She shared a receptionist and had her own office within the other firm's suite. "This lessened the blow, and even though I eventually had to move, it was still a good way to start, because it gave me an opportunity to figure out what I needed." Today, her firm, Evensky, Brown, & Katz, operates out of a nice suite in Coral Gables.

If you can't find a related company in your area, Katz says you can't do better than start with an executive suite until you figure it out. It's worth it, even if you have to move. "It's a really good idea. It doesn't cost as much as trying to staff up yourself, and you get access to a conference room—but you have your own little office."

If you are with a broker-dealer, ask them for advice. Some are even starting transitional suites—offices within their own offices—where you can get your practice rolling until you can get a place of your own. These are essentially company-sponsored executive suites, and one that I've seen is as upscale as anything a planner could hope for.

Your first office is where you figure out everything else— your clients, your growth plans, your staffing ideas. "Often, when we decide we're going to start a business, we don't really know what kind of space we're going to need," continues Katz, "because we don't know how many people we're going to need, we don't know how we're going to grow, and making that big commitment right off the bat is tough."

C *a s e* S *t u d y*
## A ROOM (OR TWO) OF HER OWN

Sophia Fitzgerald, CFP, has been working at wirehouse for years and is now ready to go it alone. She has some savings and is ready to establish a practice in her town of Baskerville, New York, a suburban bedroom village about an hour's drive outside of New York City. Her first step is deciding where she will practice.

Sophia first considers her home, where she lives with her husband, who commutes into the city, and two children, a daughter in middle school and a son who has just started high school. It's on a quiet street about three miles from the actual village. The second story of her house has an extra room that was used for slumber parties and toy train setups over the years, but has now been turned into an glorified storeroom. Sophia realizes she could clean this out and turn it into an office. It's especially attractive because the back stairs lead directly to this room. Clients wouldn't have to come across family members using the main stairs.

However, she quickly runs into drawbacks. Can the office accommodate a computer, printer, fax, scanner, and desk lamp? The house is old and might need extensive electrical work to handle so many items. Also, although the office has private stairs, it's near her children's bedrooms. She'll have to worry about loud teenagers playing their music and talking on the phone while she's trying to talk quietly to a client. Also, there are no expansion possibilities: she can fit herself and two other people, and that's it. Three clients (say, a couple and grown child) or two clients and an assistant? Out of the question.

Then there is parking. The street is too narrow for road parking. The only place to park the car is in her driveway. With her car and her husband's car, the driveway starts to get crowded. If one client shows up before she has finished with another, it's going to get very crowded. In two years, her son is going to want a car as well. And, if she found a way to fit even a part-time secretary into the office the employee will need parking space as well.

Sophia thinks that maybe someday, when the kids are off to college and she can expand into their bedrooms, a home office may work nicely. The smaller bedroom could be a reception area/second office. By then, loyal clients will be comfortable being in her home, and she won't be nervous about the normal home sounds. But right now, Sophia realizes she's better off starting with a traditional office.

She looks at options in the village proper. Baskerville is small, and except for a medical arts building, there are no appropriate office suites. However, the village boasts a few blocks of two-story buildings with shops on the bottom and offices above. A lawyer and a tax accountant have offices there, so she thinks the buildings would be appropriate for a financial planner. In fact, she visits both of them to see if they have a room they would like to sublet. She knows both professionals slightly because their children are classmates of her children. The lawyer handles wills, mortgage closings, and some litigation, and the CPA has a tax and business consulting practice, but neither does financial planning, so Sophia sees them as good sources of mutual referrals.

However, although both wish her well, neither has any extra room. In fact, their practices are thriving as Baskerville gets more and more crowded with city dwellers drawn by the pleasant neighborhood and good schools. Indeed, both professionals are wondering how long they can remain where they are without moving to larger digs. However, the lawyer gives her the card of the real estate agent who rented him his current office.

Sophia is in luck. Another office in the village, occupied by a retiring consulting engineer, has just become available. The agent shows Sophia the office and quotes her the price and terms. (Sophia later checks these against ads in the real estate section of the county newspaper to make sure they are within the norm for the area.) The office has a small anteroom/reception area with a bathroom as well as an inner office. The landlord wired the building for cable several years ago, and the local cable company provides cable Internet service, but Sophia will have to pay for that herself. The building was rewired to code recently, so there are enough outlets for all her office equipment. Both rooms already have phone jacks.

For an extra fee, the landlord will provide cleaning services. However, because Sophia's son is saving up to buy a used car when he gets a little older, she plans to hire him to clean the office on the weekends. (As the accountant would tell her, keeping it in the family will give her a nice tax break.)

The office suite is a little larger than Sophia needs right now—she is not planning to hire an assistant or receptionist for a while—but she expects she may grow and is willing to extend her resources to two rooms. The landlord will let her put a sign on the window advertising her practice.

The locale is great. The village allows two-hour parking on the street, and there is a small, first-come/first-serve private parking lot she shares with a stationery store and a florist on the ground floor. Because the malls began luring away many shoppers, the streets are not crowded on weekdays, so there are plenty of spaces. If Sophia's clientele expands beyond the greater Baskerville area, the office is also within walking distance of the commuter train lines that serve New York City and points beyond. Clients could visit her even without using a car.

Across the street is the Star of Bombay Indian restaurant ("curries our specialty"), and down the block is Alfredo's Italian restaurant ("a free glass of wine with each entrée"). Both do takeout, and both are suitable for entertaining clients. This could help with what is the only real drawback to her office: it's a walkup, which could be difficult for elderly or infirm clients. A comfortable meeting over lunch, however, could do the trick.

Sophia signs a lease and the landlord starts painting. Meanwhile, she has to furnish the office. This means a trip to IKEA, three exits away on the interstate. Sophia takes careful stock of what she will need: an L-shaped desk that can accommodate a computer and a keyboard at the proper typing level, filing cabinets, and visitor chairs for the office and the reception area. Because she doesn't have an employee yet, she buys a coffee table for the reception area but not an extra desk. The office windows are not large, so she goes with light-blond furniture that will not exaggerate the relative darkness of the office. She arranges delivery.

A weekend trip to the Metropolitan Museum of Art gift shop will give her several posters she can hang on the wall, and there is a framing store in the village.

Next come the services. She calls the cable company to open a business account and order her modem kit. A call to the phone company sets up two lines—one in the main office and one in the future receptionist's office. She gets one number with multiple lines and a voice mail system she can access from offsite.

She places an order for business cards and customized stationery with a local printer who specializes in business cards, flyers, and wedding invitations. Her neighbor florist can provide potted plants. The stationery store is happy to open up a business account for her. Sophia knows that the OfficeMax in the mall is probably cheaper, but there is an advantage to working locally, and her office needs are likely to be minimal: pens and pencils, a few pads of lined paper, good white bond for her laser printer, and some paper clips.

The CPA gives her the number of the sign painter who took care of his window; she makes an appointment. At home again, she alerts the CFP Board of Standards and the Financial Planning Association of her new address and phone number.

Is that it? Well, the sign painter is busy for two weeks. IKEA had to back order the chairs. The cable company "can't find" her order and has to put her on the bottom of the list. The painter the landlord hired is in the middle of a really messy divorce and will be spending most of the next few weeks in court.

Fortunately, Sophia expected the unexpected and did not make any appointments yet with prospective clients. But does she have any? She discovered the neighbor lawyer is concerned about college costs and wants to open a 529 plan—he needs advice on which one. The CPA is a tax whiz but admits he's weak on investments—can he drop by later to discuss what he should be doing with his retirement funds? The florist wants to talk about estate planning. The printer's wife teaches at the local elementary school and doesn't know how to allocate her 403(b) funds. No matter how busy, Sophia never forgot that everyone she meets is an potential client. On her first day, the florist leaves the shop in charge of his assistant—and becomes her first professional engagement as an independent planner in her new office.

Fortunately, IKEA delivered the chairs that morning.

# EXECUTIVE SUMMARY

- What is right for you? Home or office building? If an office building, a traditional rental or executive suite?
- Consider who you are and the image you feel comfortable with. Put yourself in the place of the clients you want to reach (covered in Chapter 3, "Know Thyself"). As Bowen says, "Before you set up an office, what is the market you're going after?"
- Take a look at your location and your options. Are you in a big city? A small city? A rural area?
- Is it even possible, because of your home and family situation, to create a home office?
- Check the Internet and Yellow Pages. Are executive suites available near you?
- Examine your budget.
- Can you imagine yourself with multiple partners—other planners and considerable support staff? Think about how you physically will grow.
- If you're affiliated with a broker-dealer, ask for their help. Some of them are starting their own temporary executive suite programs in selected cities.
- For planners with the right personality, a virtual office can save money and keep the staff happy.
- Many—probably most—planners will have to move at some point, so don't obsess over perfection.

# 2

# BITS AND BYTES

I admit that my car is ten years old, but aside from a broken tape deck and a few dings, it runs fine. It doesn't look odd—no one points and says, "look at that weird, old-fashioned car." But a ten-year-old computer belongs in the Smithsonian. Even a three-year-old desktop probably won't do what you need it to do. I initially was going to give a lot of specific advice in this chapter, but in the interval between the writing and the publishing, the material would become dated.

Of course, I could simply tell you to buy what I have, an AMD Athlon XP processor, 512 MB DDR SDRAM memory, USB 2.0 ports and Firewire . . .

Are you still with me?

Don't worry—none of this will be on the final. You may fear that technology is all about jargon, but it's not. Technology is about saving time and money. It's about making a big practice out of a small one or making a small one run more profitably. It's about doing what you want to do and not what you have to do. It's about working in your office or your living room or in an office in a backyard hammock. It is not about spending time managing your computer—if that's happened, then you're doing it wrong. It's about your computer managing your professional life.

You have to take responsibility for your technology education, however, and this chapter is your first step. There are some great resources (see the Resources), but no one text will tell you everything you need to know. Don't let some helpful sales clerk sell you a 700-page book on getting the most out of Microsoft Outlook. You're wasting your money and time and probably risking your sanity, because you don't need to know everything there is to know about Outlook. Technology changes so quickly that any book will be too dated to give you current advice on what to buy.

You also have to know what you are never going to be able to do yourself: setting up wireless networks, connecting a multi-office staff, or setting up a broadband Internet connection. You will need outside help—consultants and various vendors—to achieve some things. But I'm going to explain those, too.

Getting back to my ten-year-old car and another automobile analogy, this chapter will teach you the computer equivalents of how to shop for a car in the lot, pump your own gas, change your own oil, and fix a flat. It will give you the technical details that will let you talk intelligently with a mechanic. It will *not* teach you how to fix your transmission. It would take forever for me to explain, and you have better things to do.

"Technology is a hit-or-miss situation, a vicious cycle," says Nancy Langdon Jones. "You need the Internet to research the products, but by the time you get them, they're outdated, so you have to research some more. That's the biggest business expense—keeping up with things. Yet it's absolutely necessary—you can't do without it."

Deena Katz sums it up quickly: "Technology is a monster." But it can be tamed and make a difference between a successful practice and a failure. Especially if you're taking the home office route, a basic knowledge of technology will make your practice not merely more efficient, but possible.

## BEGIN AT THE BEGINNING

The first thing you want and need is a desktop computer with a printer. The difference between a powerful machine and a merely adequate one is only a few hundred dollars, so think big. Many computers come preloaded with standard Microsoft products: Word, Excel, Outlook (for e-mail), and PowerPoint. These are standard; every planner needs these.

Still, there's no need to be wasteful. The best guide for purchasing a computer appears in *The Wall Street Journal*. Technology columnist Walt Mossberg periodically addresses what you need—and don't need—in a computer, and his Thursday column should be mandatory reading for every planner. For example, he discusses chip speed and manufacturers' insistence that bigger is better. In fact, beyond a certain point, you will pay extra money for no more extra performance. (Will a Porsche get you to your office faster than a Toyota? Not if your town's speed limit is 40 miles per hour.)

Another source is the companies you work with. If you're affiliated with a broker-dealer, they will provide much of your software and may have some good advice on systems. The same is true for a custodian you work with as an investment advisor. For example, TD Waterhouse is making Advent software available to its affiliated advisers at a fraction of the list price. Waterhouse, as well as other major custodians, also has proprietary software that can prove invaluable.

Before I get into more details, I'll add a word on Macintosh versus Windows machines. I'm going to earn the wrath of a lot of fanatical Mac fans, but I'm going to recommend strongly that you stick with well-known computers that run Microsoft

Windows such as Dell, Hewlett-Packard, and Compaq. It's not that Macs aren't great machines, but they never caught on in the financial world. Some software you want simply will be unavailable in Mac formats, and you'll find yourself alone when trying to get help from colleagues. In fact, I was planning to write an article on Windows versus Mac for financial planning, but I couldn't find a single financial planner who uses a Mac.

## THE ON-RAMP TO THE INFORMATION HIGHWAY

Speaking specifically to planners, John Olsen, probably the most tech-savvy planner I've met, has some specific advice: "There are some tech rules you better learn."

The first rule, says Olsen, is to get a fast Internet connection. The slowest connection, available to anyone, is a simple dial-up. That is, you plug your computer into a standard phone jack and have it dial a phone number to connect. This system is also called POTS, for Plain Old Telephone System. Any computer you get will have an internal modem that will let you do this.

However, POTS is too slow for a proper office set up. Go for one of several high-speed options, generally known as *broadband*. Your choice will depend on your location and what local phone companies provide: DSL, T-1, and T-3 connections are some of the most common services. The technical differences are not important. (I never got a good explanation of why there is not T-2.) But get something. As Olsen says, "You can't have a modem fast enough. It is not possible to have a download speed that's too fast." Ask your local telephone company what is available in your area.

One of your best options, if it's available in your area, is a cable modem. This is an inexpensive yet extremely fast connection through the same cable that plugs into your television. If you already have cable in your home, the setup is quick and simple. In fact, the service is likely offered through the same company. You need a special cable modem, which is about the size of this book, that connects to the cable coming out of your wall. The computer connects to this modem with a special cable that looks like a phone line but is actually a little wider. If you have a late-model machine, it will have the necessary outlet, or *port,* built in, ready to connect to a cable modem.

"I have a cable modem, and when it's down, I'm not a happy camper," says Olsen. "You need to understand just how important a fast connection is." For example, if you are affiliated with a broker-dealer, the firm may send you updated software over the Internet. "ING, for example, has a wonderful illustration software, but it's updated every month online. Downloading the updates takes forever with a standard telephone connection."

Don't make the mistake of thinking that your clients don't spend a lot of time online or don't work with e-mail, or that they're too old to learn to use e-mail or visit your Web site. Everyone is online today—retirees more than anyone, because they're staying in touch with their grandchildren.

## FACE-TO-FACE WITH THE MACHINE

Another area not to stint on, according to Olsen, is the monitor. "It's not possible to have a monitor that's too big. Or that's too clear." Get at least a 19″ flatscreen monitor. It's expensive, but you're spending a good part of your life in front of it. "Treat your eyes, treat your body, treat your soul—go out and get one." These also take up a lot less room on your desk.

Mark Calhoun, a technology consultant to financial professionals, concurs. "With desktop systems, the hardware is so cheap today, you might as well get the best. Consider getting two monitors for each desktop, in fact. You can be viewing different things on one computer at the same time—you can have a Web site and your contact manager open and visible." (I went insane with jealousy when I found out a colleague at Reuters had two monitors.)

He also suggests getting rid of the desktop machine altogether and buying just a laptop with a docking station. This allows you to slide the laptop into a rack-like "station" that automatically connects to a full-sized keyboard, monitor and printer, giving you desktop size with laptop convenience. However, when you leave at the end of the day, you can take all the files with you without copying them onto another machine. "They're cheap and powerful and extremely convenient—you can work from anywhere."

## LOOKING AT THE RESULTS

Every planner needs a black and white laser printer. Color laser printers are still expensive but are falling in price all the time. If you like printing reports with color graphs in them, consider springing for one. However, if you have a Kinko's or similar printer in your town, you can hand them a disk and have them print your document on their high-end color printers.

Color ink-jet printers are economical, but you may not be happy with the print quality when it comes to client documents. Again, *The Wall Street Journal* is a great source of new product info, as is *The New York Times*, which also covers technology on Thursdays. You're going to have to rely on newspapers and magazines for information on what is available and what you can afford. Again, books just date too quickly to be of use.

## BACK UP AND AVOID DISASTER

The SEC and NASD have strict rules for electronically storing and backing up client records (see the section later in this chapter on starting a paperless office). You need to review these with a compliance authority. However, in general, saving your data has become easy. Make sure you buy a computer that can create, or *burn*, CDs. These are inexpensive, quick, and fairly permanent media for backing up a range of material. This entire book took up just a small portion of one CD, for example.

Another option is an Iomega Zip or Jaz drive, which uses special reusable disks. These probably do not meet compliance standards, because they easily can be erased and reused, but this feature actually makes them particularly useful for ordinary back-up tasks. These disks fit into special drives that can be detached easily and carried to another computer, making them a handy portable device for transferring material from one computer to another.

There are also services that automatically back up your files, over the Internet, to a remote server. These are noted in the Resources. For larger systems, there are digital tape drives. But compliance rules aside, do *not* have the sole copies of your key files in one computer. Consider which files are essential to the smooth running of your practice—from address books to client profiles to financial and human resources data—and back it up at least once a week. Some people just take the back-up tapes or disks home. Others keep them in a bank's safe-deposit box. But do something.

## TECHNOLOGY THAT HELPS YOU BECOME BIG . . .

That's just the basics. To get the most out of technology, so technology can help you grow and, indeed, be the *reason* you can grow, you are going to have to learn more and eventually connect with experts—either outside consultants or in-house managers.

"Starting out, it's just you, and it's not a big deal," says Katz. "But as soon as you have an assistant, you're going to want to be connected." That is, *networked*. You're going to need help with this—local help. "Start asking around," suggests Katz. "Find out which consultants other firms in your area are using. Get someone who knows your business." Katz found a company that works in her area with small business owners. "They came in and networked us, then grew with us. As we got bigger, they made different changes. We were able to manage technology growth with people who have been with us for a long time. So we really looked hard right off the bat for somebody who was going to give us good service and who was going to be around and who really understood small business."

Such services aren't free, but the costs become easier to bear when you look at your practice like a business. Says Calhoun, "A lot of our clients view every dollar that they spend as a dollar out of their pockets. Others view their practice as a business—even if it's just them—so they're making investments when they spend money." And technology will be an investment, because it certainly isn't going to be your core competency.

"Get rid of everything you're not going to make money on," says Calhoun. "In other words, outsource it." For example, one of Calhoun's recent clients is a wirehouse rep who just left to go independent. "His old employer did everything for him. As a service provider, we can provide the same or similar services." In fact, Calhoun's firm, Etelligent Consulting, will even take care of billing and reporting.

Ross Levin isn't wasting his time managing the technology of his practice. However, he has reached the point where he can have a full-time technology manager on staff. Still, he warns it's not a perfect solution. "The hardest part is managing someone like that. The personality of a technology person is so different from the personalities of everyone else we work with. Now we have a really good person in the role that does a great job. But we actually brought in a tech project manager just to manage our technology guy, as a consultant." Essentially, this person provides a bridge between what Levin's firm needs and what is possible.

As you get bigger, you will want to customize, that is, rely more on programs written just for you and less on off-the-shelf solutions. Customization is a double-edged sword. "One of the problems with doing your own database and similar items is that it's very hard to blow it up if you don't like it," says Levin, who has now found software that may work better than what he currently has. However, it doesn't have all the custom solutions his current product does. "We've been spoiled by what we have. There are certain things that our database does that no other database could do—items exclusive for our practice."

Still, going outside for anything beyond the desktop basics is the recommended path for most larger firms. "We went outside for tech—of course!" says Sheryl Garrett. "We're *planners.* We're not good business operators, we're not good marketers, and we're definitely not computer experts. We shouldn't even try." She also found a local consultant to handle networking and programming, and he makes house calls: "In any kind of emergency, I can pick up the phone and call him anytime, night or day. He fixed a virus right away. You need someone who can drop everything and come running."

No, it isn't easy to find someone like this. So start looking now before you have a serious problem. Ask friends and colleagues. Try the Yellow Pages. Some CompUSA outlets have training, for example. Garrett was also fortunate enough to find what she calls a technology coach. "He will do things like teach us how to get the most out of Microsoft's Outlook or set up a paperless office—tasks that can enhance productivity."

Lou Stanasolovich has experimented, using a multiprong approach to his technology problems. He found that if you have someone dedicated, you don't necessarily need a well-trained authority. "We had an employee who had been with us for about four years. She wasn't a trained technology person and didn't even have a college degree, but she was extremely curious about how things worked and ended up saving us tens of thousands in consulting costs."

One larger company designated a tech expert in each department, someone who had an interest in and facility for tech support. This person was then sent to additional training to become a first line of defense when a problem cropped up, freeing the full-time tech support staff for more complex problems.

Consider the economics of technology consulting—the weekly salary of a curious, full-time employee, Stanasolovich found, is equal to only 14 hours a week of a trained consultant's time. Ask yourself what a motivated and interested employee could do. "In the end, I think you need a combination of staff and a tech expert. And we're learning that fast—an employee who is technically astute but not necessarily a technology expert, plus someone who is an expert."

All these firms have no more than about 20 staff members. Most have less, and you probably will never get as large as Ric Edelman with his 90 employees and his $2 billion under management. But, big or small, the way you handle technology is the same. Give it to a consultant. Give it to a dedicated staff member. But don't do it yourself. Edelman has an IT staff of seven. "Technology is a tremendous tool to support the client service needs that we have. We've even developed a lot of our software and systems in-house and customize off-the-shelf software. I have four programmers who do nothing but develop systems for us. We spend a lot of money on those types of things—I'm a big believer that it's a good investment."

## . . . AND TECHNOLOGY THAT HELPS YOU STAY SMALL

Don't make the mistake, however, of thinking that technology has no surprises or assistance for the firm that wants to stay small—or that you can just ignore the issue. In fact, technology can make a small firm work. Small-town planner Amy Leavitt had to make do with what was available in a rural area, so she leaned as much as possible on her broker-dealer, Lincoln/ Sagemark. She installed the firm's proprietary software and wasn't shy about asking Lincoln's advice and assistance in setting up her system. Your broker-dealer doesn't succeed unless you do, so ask them for help. Once she was established and able to hire staff, "I hired people who were more tech-oriented than I was."

Morris Armstrong, who doesn't have any staff at all, initially admitted to owning nothing more complex than an abacus. Actually, he has a new Dell desktop, which, at 512 MB, is pretty much as powerful as any planner needs. (Some planners have even made computers do the work of a fax machine, thanks to a program called e Fax <www.efax.com>. At a very modest cost, this allows users to send and receive faxes from a desktop computer, through the Internet, with a special phone number.)

He invested in a moderately priced Adobe product <www .adobe.com> that lets him create PDF files. These are professional looking, well-designed documents that anyone can access with a free reader program. "All my Word docs and Excel spreadsheets can be turned into PDFs for client use. They can read them but can't change them. Many of my disclosure documents are also PDF, and I can upload them to a Web site. It was well worth it." They are easy to transmit by e-mail, a fact Armstrong appreciates.

Nancy Jones feels pretty tech savvy today, but she didn't start that way. "It was something I had to teach myself." She got some help, in fact, from fellow planner John Olsen, as well as from planning tech gurus Joel Bruckenstein and David Drucker, whose essential works are covered in the Resources. "I try to educate myself and keep up with what's going on."

Jones highlighted the problem of finding good companies to partner with. "So many tech companies go out of business—right away." Although today, national entities like AOL, MSN, and cable companies dominate the Internet connection market, there was a time when small, local companies would provide connections just for one city or town. The word was you got better service. "For our Internet connection, we tried a local provider who was right in our community."

But they went bankrupt. So she went with stable, national provider Earthlink. Eventually DSL came to her town, making the choices even more complex. DSL provider GTE (now Verizon) had a broadband monopoly in the neighborhood. It threatened to charge an installation fee for each of her five computers if she stayed with Earthlink. However, her tech consultant eventually found another provider—again a local company—that helped arrange the basic GTE-DSL service with the cost of just one connection.

The moral of the story is that getting online is still a growing, changing, and complex field. Getting a high-speed connection is not yet as simple as getting a new phone line. Be patient and don't expect to be up-to-speed—literally or figuratively—right away.

## TRIUMPH OF THE SMALL

Connecting is just the beginning. Check with your broker-dealer or compliance consultant—you can now store many of your essential records on CDs. As noted above, you can burn your own CDs. These are suitable not only for back ups but for a whole range of tasks because CD burners have become standard equipment on most new desktop computers. File cabinets disappear—and so do hours wasted finding something in a folder. Instead, do an electronic search on your digitally stored client files. You will never lose anything again.

Also, some clients may accept, and actually prefer, presentations and plans on a CD. These can be in addition to or even instead of a printed document. You can also buy label kits that let you put your firm name and logo on the CD.

In fact, technology can replace more than you know, making a one-person shop a smooth, efficient—and highly profitable—venture.

The local carpenter my wife and I hired to fix some doors in our elderly house left us his bill *typed on a manual typewriter.* Many smaller planners think that's what practicing small means—planning by day, then staying up at night to type invoices, folding brochures to mail in envelopes that jam your printer anyway, and sifting through all the phone messages you couldn't get to during the workday.

It doesn't have to be that way. Much of the theme of this book is outsourcing—getting someone outside your firm to do what you don't do best, so you can stick to being a financial planner. Well, technology, at its highest level, is an internal outsourcing solution. You effectively outsource work to your desktop, your software, and various gadgets.

Technology is not a solution just for supergeeks or for millionaires who can afford James Bond gizmos. A vanguard of small planners has already figured out how to squeeze every drop of efficiency out of technology. These solutions are applicable to firms of all sizes, but for the very smallest firms, for those who work alone, the information in this book is what you have to know to stay competitive. It's what you have to know to increase the margin of profitability.

No one knows more about doing this than Olsen, whose expertise runs far beyond getting a fast machine with a big screen. He does financial and estate planning, sells life insurance, consults with other professional advisors, and consults on software, in addition to doing writing and public speaking. He does all this with no staff, not even a part-time assistant. He is successful, not because he knows what it means to have a 2.0 MHZ processor, but because he *gets* technology. This is not rocket science. All you need is the right attitude, and you too can *get* it.

# BUY A PDA—BUY IT ALL

A personal digital assistant (PDA), also known by the brand name Palm Pilot, is a handheld computer usually just small enough to fit into the inside pocket of a man's suit jacket. Basic functions include a contact manager (a detailed address database) and address book, to-do list, and memo pad. You can enter data with a plastic *stylus,* and a cable lets you quickly and easily back up information onto one or more computers in a process called *synching.* In fact, when you're at your desktop computer, you can enter and change information in a big-screen version of your PDA's display, and when you synch, the PDA software makes sure the desktop and handheld information are copied onto each other.

I have my PDA with me all the time, but when I go to the NAPFA's and the FPA's national conferences as well as the AICPA financial planning conferences, I rarely see them on other planners.

John Olsen, who swears by his PDA, thinks that's a pity.

"People kid me and they say, 'Well you just love your toys—you're a tech guy. You love technology.' But I tell them, 'No, I don't love technology. I love what technology allows me to do with my life.' And that's a big difference. I'm not a geek!"

So you have to change your mindset. One of Olsen's leading frustrations, in fact, is that he feels people don't see innovation as leading to productivity, and that's what you need to do to run your firm like a business.

Consider a mutual fund or an insurance company offering new products, says Olsen. "We immediately see the impact of that change on our practice. But when someone gives us a tool that lets us do what we were doing faster or more efficiently or both, we relegate it to that room in our heads we call 'technological geek stuff.' We don't translate it into, 'This is about how I work. This is about my practice. This is about my life, my professional life.'"

Maybe the profession is made up of technophobes. But it doesn't have to be that way, and you can't afford to ignore the productivity changes wrought by PDAs and other items. "You can't just decide whether you want to integrate new technology. It's like wondering whether you want to integrate a new tax law!" One wonders about which 19th-century banks bought phone systems first—and which thought it was just a fad.

So understand Olsen's frustration when he's relegated to the group "with pocket protectors and adhesive tape on their glasses." Other planners have said to him, "Oh, is that a PDA? That's nice for you guys. But I'm a salesperson. I'm out there seeing people." Olsen just wants to say, "Your PDA will allow you to see people *and* have something better to say to them when you see them. Isn't that what it's all about?"

So what does Olsen's PDA let him do?

When Olsen is out on the golf course, a client can reach him and ask, "How is my IRA coming?" His PDA has it right there: what the client put in, and what the tax basis would have been. The PDA lets Olsen keep in touch. He can even automatically download from DST or another aggregator using E-Z Data's client data system. Of course, if Olsen worked in a larger firm, someone else at the office might have been reachable. But he practices alone, and technology lets him.

He can easily download magazine articles on to his PDA and read them at any time. (See the Resources at the end of this book for details.) "I give a presentation on how to achieve a 25-hour day, and I ask the attendees how many are behind on reading their journals. Everybody raises their hands. We're all behind. Now, how many in the course of their day either go to lunch or wait for a bus or a spouse—you have dead time. Everyone does. Would you like to turn that into time you can read your journal without having to have a hard copy?"

I have a journalist trick that I do with my PDA, and you, too, can use this for your contacts. I collect dozens of business cards when I go to conferences. Later, on the flight home or whenever I have a few minutes, I enter all the information into my PDA, including notes on how I met them and what we talked about. Months later, we may meet again, and if their name is familiar, I can just call them up on my PDA before reintroducing myself and say, "I remember you, Joe—we met in Chicago last year and talked about that new line of no-load funds."

They think I have the world's greatest memory. But you can even take it a step further, with a PDA that has a digital camera and lets you associate photos with contacts.

With additional software and add-ons, your PDA can virtually replace a laptop computer at a fraction of the cost and size. You can't use it for big projects, but it can take care of many tasks formerly assigned to a full-fledged laptop or desktop. It can be cumbersome to add a lot of copy with the stylus, but you can buy portable keyboards that attach to the PDA. Additional programs let you read and edit Word and Excel documents as well as other standard document formats.

Increasingly, PDAs are coming with wireless capabilities, allowing you to get and receive e-mail. The Treo, from PalmOne, has merged the cell phone with the PDA, and it's gotten some nice write-ups from technology reviewers.

If your off-site e-mail isn't that critical to you (and most of us can wait until we get to a hotel to check our e-mail), some programs allow you to download e-mail from your program when you synch it with your main computer, respond to it offline while you're on the commuter train home, and have it sent when you synch in your office the next morning. It's full e-mail management—except the actual sending and receiving.

For planners who like the idea of being able to grow without hiring a lot of staff, John Bowen also has a great model. With a little research, he's found a technological solution to just about everything, even though he is not in a major urban center. As noted previously, Bowen works out of his home, and technology has made this possible.

"I'm in a country setting—I have the equivalent broadband access of a wireless T1 that costs $200 month. I also have a Blackberry." The fancifully named Blackberry is a souped-up version of those little beepers doctors always carry around. They let you receive and send e-mails and, in some instances, phone calls. Originally introduced to coordinate with large corporate e-mail systems, they are becoming more popular with small firms as well.

In addition, Bowen has a wireless connection added to his laptop. "That way, I can work by the pool and still get my e-mails. I've found that you can be as connected as you want to be."

Like Olsen, you don't need an assistant, or, like Bowen, you can have one but not necessarily in the same office or even in the same time zone. Bowen is in Northern California. His assistant is in Atlanta. "When someone leaves me a voice mail, it is actually translated into an e-mail—an electronic sound file. I can check it on the phone or get it as e-mail that I can forward to my assistant or simply listen to it on the computer."

In fact, the line between speaking and typing is disappearing, thanks to increasingly sophisticated voice-recognition software. Bowen can dictate his letters and anything else with Dragon Naturally Speaking voice recognition software. You simply speak into a computer and watch the words appear on the screen. He also uses transcription services—these are nationwide companies that allow you to upload a sound file or just dictate over a phone for as little as a penny a word.

Olsen, in fact, was planning to buy a digital voice recorder that comes with Dragon voice recognition software. "Five days a week I go to the fitness club at the Ritz Carlton. Then it's downstairs to the cigar club, where I can have a smoke and dictate. I put the file, which is at least 95 percent accurate, into my desktop when I get home and open it as a Word file."

What's the net result of increasing your technology use? You have more time with clients and more time for planning activities. Admits Olsen, "I define myself as a lazy guy who wants to get the job done. So that's why I use these tools. They enable me to be a lot more productive."

## WHERE DOES THIS ALL LEAD?

You may worry about what happens as you add more and more technology to your life, and you're right—you need to watch out. My wife and I visited a gadget-obsessed relative: he had the latest flat-screen TV on the wall, which was hooked into a DVD player, VCR, CD player, video game, and satellite connection. Only we couldn't turn it on. That's right—it was such a complex system we couldn't get it to work. Don't let this happen to you. Add slowly and carefully to your technological suite, working with consultants and vendors as needed, so you understand what you have.

You may reach a point where virtually every piece of paper disappears from your offices. Everything is digital. Every file. Every client record. Every marketing initiative. It's all digital. It's possible, and someday it may be common—and then essential.

The last technical barrier to the paperless office was regulatory, but in recent years, the NASD and SEC have allowed planners to store key files on certain permanent media, like CDs. So in theory, you can eliminate all paper. You will need some solid technology partners and the full cooperation of your broker-dealer, if you're affiliated with one, and any compliance consultants you work with.

Getting started on developing a completely paperless office is not easy. Although many documents today are electronic, many still originate as paper. One of the most expensive and complex tasks in becoming paperless is scanning the paper documents into your computer and organizing the digital documents. You need a scanner and optical character recognition (OCR) software, which often comes with the scanner. Just scanning a page into a computer isn't enough—the computer will treat the document as a picture, and you won't be able to edit it or even search for words on it. OCR software tells your scanner to read the document, so it becomes an editable document on your machine.

Although scanners are now available for so little that even the smallest office can afford one, you will need something large and robust if you want a paperless office. But with the right equipment, paperless is possible, as Sharon Kayfetz showed. A paperless pioneer, she actually managed to get rid of every piece of paper in her office. All her client records are stored on her laptop and backed up onto CDs. An initial technology investment can be substantial, but as the need for an office and staff disappears, the cost savings can be huge.

"When our firm first did some research on cost, we saw that the price of moving to a paperless office was just outlandish. The first quote we got was running $50,000 to $60,000, through one of the larger scanner manufacturers." However, she was able to team up with LaserFiche, which not only provides the technology necessary for high-speed, accurate scanning but promises to do so in a way that satisfied stringent regulatory requirements. "Eventually, we were able to move out of our retail space entirely."

Think of it as a process, advises Kayfetz. "It's something you really have to talk and think about. You have to have a plan of what you're going to be doing. Because if you don't, you'll get into a lot of trouble. How do you set up your filing system? What gets scanned first? What doesn't have to be scanned? What do you need OCR for and what can be scanned without it? You need a plan—a plan to change office tech."

The whole office has to be on board with paperless. Not everyone can handle this psychologically. The advantages to clients can be enormous. Kayfetz was able to do planning at her clients' homes—a luxury they appreciated—because she had all their records, necessary forms, and investment history stored on a series of CDs. (Laptop hard disks and Internet facilities can also store data.) But not every client was comfortable with this, although Kayfetz said only one of her hundreds of clients left the practice when her firm switched to paperless.

Someday, everyone may practice without paper. Right now, however, most aim for the *almost* paperless office. Even reducing most of your paper is a big savings—electronic files are easier to store and find and take less room. Olsen has achieved this with another program called PaperMaster, which coordinates scanning and creates a virtual filing cabinet right on his computer.

"Whenever I get important paper documents, I just scan them into the folder where they belong. I can tell the built-in OCR software to go through a whole filing cabinet and do an OCR scan on all of them. So when I try to find something and can't remember where I put it, I can do a keyword search and find every document with that word." This process also saves Olsen time spent filling out forms. "For example, take a new accounts form from my broker-dealer. I scan it into my computer with PaperMaster, and now there's a blank template I can fill out on my computer, instead of by hand." He can even fax it directly to his broker-dealer from the computer, without having to print it out.

The bottom line on paperless? It's a process, not something you start out with. Technology will reduce your paper from day one, but don't expect to go completely paperless until you are comfortable with your technology generally. More than any other tech task, this one requires a solid technology partner like LaserFiche. Don't be upset if you never become completely paperless—getting even halfway there is an enormous achievement.

## ASSET MANAGEMENT SOFTWARE: A BRIEF WORD

If managing assets is part of your practice, you will have to pick software to help you do this. You can always switch later, but it's a major hassle. Many advisors have admitted sticking for years with a package they hated, even a package they knew was being phased out, rather than switch.

After some buyouts and competitive fights, two major suites were left standing: Centerpiece, owned by leading custodian Charles Schwab; and Advent, an independent, publicly held company that also owns Techfi, a formerly independent package Advent bought out.

Each suite has its champions and detractors. Beyond the technology advantages one may have over the other are political issues. Schwab has toyed over time with restricting access to Centerpiece to those who custody funds with them. Meanwhile, as noted above, Schwab challenger TD Waterhouse has a deal to provide a vastly discounted Advent package to its advisors. By the time you read this, there may be another deal, another wrinkle, and, possibly, another choice.

Try not to get caught in the hype. For example, you may find Microsoft, Bill Gates, and Steve Ballmer objectionable, and you may be right about them. But you're stuck with Microsoft products, and some of them are very, very good, so you make the best of it.

It's the same thing with Advent and Centerpiece and, probably, any rival that crops up. Corporate behavior can be sneaky, bullying, and weaselly, but the packages can be very, very good. Make a choice that fits the way you practice, and don't base it on your objections to overzealous corporate marketing. Make a rational decision, not an emotional one.

To get clear guidance, get some advice from your custodian— Schwab, Waterhouse, or whomever—and see if they have a deal on price. At the very least, confirm with your custodian that the software you're thinking of interfaces neatly with their data. You don't want to spend your days trying to force your software and your custodian's data system to talk to each other.

Call the software companies yourself and ask them to describe their product's features. Can they give you a demo? What kind of support will they provide? Some have training classes, even periodic training conferences in different parts of the country. Software packages are expensive, so software companies should be at least as solicitous of you as a car salesperson and just as upfront with options. (Expect them to be just as pushy.)

On your part, be honest with the companies—and with yourself—about the assets you have under management or may expect to have in the coming few years. Some software packages are scaled based on your assets under management. As the assets increase, so does your fee, sometimes dramatically. At the other end, custodians have been known to cut bigger breaks on software for their biggest advisors, so that as you grow, your fee would shrink.

Think of your asset management software decision as being on par with a house purchase. No, it isn't irrevocable, but do you really want to pack up all your dishes again? It's worth some research and, most importantly, a talk with other advisors. Ask your custodian to put you in touch with other advisors with practices similar to yours and find out what their experiences have been.

## NOW YOU'RE SET

Properly researched and maintained, your technology will keep the back office of your practice running smoothly so you are free to do the brain work: crafting plans and talking to clients.

One final car analogy. You don't think about your car, about whether your transmission will work or if the wipers will operate. Periodically, you make sure the oil is changed and the tires are rotated. Every few years you may buy a new one. You take occasional care of your car, and it gets you effortlessly to your office each morning for years without another thought.

Likewise your computer.

# WEB IT

Once you're in a good position internally, you can start looking outward and get yourself a Web site. This process is fascinating and maddening. A good site will help you serve current clients and troll for new ones. But, if you let it, it can suck every minute out of your life and every dime out of your wallet.

I was privileged to cover business and technology in the early days of the Web, when small financial service firms were just beginning to explore it. I found a lot of astonishing experiments: sites with music, bizarre animated graphics, and color palettes that could induce headaches if you stared at the site too long. Most of them were homemade with simple, off-the-shelf design programs. Some of them were useful, but the vast majority had little value except as novelties.

One of the best in that early era came from pioneer Carolyn Sechler, whose virtual office was discussed in Chapter 1. Possibly the first CPA to have a Web site <www.azcpa.com>, she realized that it could brand her quickly and effectively as a cutting-edge practitioner. It brought her well-deserved national attention.

But even the weak sites established a presence and marked their creators as forward-thinking, tech-savvy practitioners. In that sense, they were big steps forward for the profession and the Web generally.

Today, that's not enough. You have to have a useful Web site that is clear and helpful—and economical. You have to walk a fine line: you *cannot* create your own Web site—this is the equivalent of fixing your own transmission—but you don't want to go overboard with consultants. I created my own Web site some years ago to teach myself programming (and to take a break from the tedious article my editor thought I was writing while I was playing online). It cost me about $20. That's why I was overwhelmed when I heard about some big corporation shelling out millions for a site that didn't even work properly. I asked in a technology chatroom how anyone could spend seven figures on a Web site. "That's easy," was one reply, "they had *consultants.*"

However, if you have an idea of what you want to accomplish, you can work effectively with a consultant to build a site that reflects your firm's personality at an affordable price.

Here are some of the tasks a Web site can take care of.

- Describe and brand your firm
- Provide profiles of you and your employees
- Explain your compensation arrangements
- Display various regulatory disclosures
- Dispense generic financial advice in the form of articles
- Explain any other aspect of your firm that otherwise would require a time-consuming phone call
- Provide a secure way for clients to view their accounts

Here's what a Web site should not do.

- Serve as your sole or chief marketing initiative
- Replace personal client contact
- Make a design "statement" at the expense of usability
- Contain so much graphics that it takes forever to load

These goals are achievable. "Web sites are pretty simple," says Mark Calhoun, "but you want it to look decent. There are some good consultants out there, and you don't have to spend a lot." Sheryl Garrett says she uses her site to its fullest. Because she runs a network of planners in addition to her own practice, she relies especially heavily on her site. "Many consumers are going to the Web site to find a planner."

Lou Stanasolovich really pushed the envelope. With a little money and effort, you can get your name pushed to the top of the results list at key search engines. "We hired a consultant to do this for us, and we've actually gotten prospective clients through our site." He says he can attribute more than $90,000 in revenue last year to his Web site because of clients who found him online. Then, assuming they continue as clients, that revenue stream will just grow and grow. "We just picked up a client who ended up paying us a $24,000 fee, and that came from the Internet. People don't believe you can do that, but we do it all the time."

Stanasolovich's site shows another swing of the pendulum. First, the Internet was going to change completely the way we bought products and services. Then, all the sites that were going to rewrite the rules scaled back drastically or disappeared altogether. Now, we're back to a healthy middle ground, where the Web can do a lot, just not everything. It can't make you a multimillionaire overnight, but it can support and grow your business.

But who can help you do this? As with other technology consulting, you can find someone local. However, one New York consultant has become the go-to guy for financial planner Web sites all over the country: Andy Gluck, of AdvisorSites. Lou Stanasolovich, Sheryl Garrett, and Deena Katz are just a few of his clients.

Although Gluck sells a budget template Web site, he strongly suggests advisors consider investing in a custom Web site— it's much more individualized, and most advisors can afford one.

The chief advantage of a custom site is that it forces advisors to think long and hard about their image and how they explain their value proposition. Gluck says your Web site isn't about HTML—the principal programming language of the Web—and it's not even about technology. "The web development process is really a way of figuring out the best way to tell people how you can help them," says Gluck. "What do you want on your home page? What is your main marketing message? How do you want to present yourself to the world? Building a custom Web site designed around your marketing message and your unique way of practicing forces you to organize your thoughts about your marketing effort."

Gluck says that the Web is a good medium for developing your marketing message. That's because it allows advisors to work remotely with designers. Also, he says the Web is a "flexible medium," meaning that it allows for easy, inexpensive changes to your marketing message—unlike a print brochure, which could result in discarding hundreds of copies when you want to make a change.

Gluck says a key element of designing your own Web site is your marketing copy. Gluck, whose firm includes a staff of experienced financial writers and editors, says most advisors write their own brochure text, but that is a mistake. "While it's good for an advisor to write the first draft of his marketing brochure, it's really important to get the help of a professional financial writer to smooth out the message and make it reader-friendly," he says. "Then, you should have that edited by another professional writer." Too often, Gluck says, advisors write their own brochure and they think it's great when actually it doesn't clearly explain how they can help people who hire them or their unique way of practicing.

"Once you have a few hundred words of marketing text that explains clearly what you do, you can probably boil it down to a four or five word slogan," says Gluck. "You then have a slogan all of a sudden, and that will make it easier for you to create a logo if you don't already have one." A logo helps an advisor create a visual corporate identity.

"Your logo, slogan, and main marketing message will help drive the design of a custom Web site," says Gluck. "Since advisors usually have an evolving marketing message, custom designing a site presents an opportunity to take your marketing message to the next level." Gluck says a template Web site doesn't force an advisor to think through marketing issues and how you want to explain your practice. "You have to walk through the introspective process of how to brand your company," he says.

For example, Gluck discusses a recent project for a financial planner: "The planner told my artists that he wanted something reminiscent of the craft movement. He said he wanted to be his clients' financial architect. So we came up with several logo compositions that represented those ideas, including a stained-glass logo and one with an architect's blueprint in the background. This process forced the adviser to think about it. Then, we created a Web site around those ideas, but it all started with marketing copy and the logo."

Your Web site should reflect you, your brand, and your unique way of giving financial advice. For example, Deena Katz's site shows images from the firm's Florida locale and people enjoying a day at the beach.

As Gluck says, "You became independent for a reason. You have unique qualities you want to tell people about. They need to capture that in text and in graphics."

Your Web site also needs content, and Gluck can provide that, too. He and his staff write articles of interest to your clients, which are uploaded on sites for you. AdvisorSites makes hundreds of articles available for posting on an advisor's web site, and advisors use a simple administration tool to pick the stories they want to appear on their Web site. "Every advisor thinks he's going to make time and prepare his own copy, but they never do it," says Gluck.

To encourage clients and prospects to visit your site, Advisor-Sites's platform allows advisors to e-mail newsletters using the articles. "Someone comes to your site, clicks on a newsletter icon, and a browser window pops inviting the reader to subscribe to your email newsletter." The advisor can control different newsletters for different client groups and pick the articles that appear in the e-mail newsletter. Every Friday, a weekly market update summarizing the stock market's activity for the previous week can be sent as an e-mail newsletter. All e-mail newsletters are branded to include the advisor's logo and allow recipients to unsubscribe at any time.

AdvisorProducts offers adjunct programs as well, such as a Web conferencing tool that lets you share documents with clients in a virtual meeting. (It's similar to WebEx, says Gluck, but much less expensive.) There's also a client survey tool, to help planners get a sense of whether their clients like them. If your broker-dealer or custodian has a system to handle it, you may be able to add a page that allows your clients to view their data securely.

Andy Gluck's AdvisorSites may not be the only game in town, but he knows what planners need, and you shouldn't move to the Web without checking out what his company can do for you. It's safe to say that today, every planner should have a Web site. Don't believe your clients aren't Web savvy, even if you mostly serve retirees. "Older people are especially comfortable on the Web. How do you think they're talking to their grandchildren?" asks Gluck. "They're chatting on AOL!"

Go to Gluck's site—he has a list of some of the sites he has designed. Also, the Introduction lists the Web site of every planner quoted in this book. Pretty much all of them have the list of "musts" (see above). Today's top advisors know that the Web is no longer the sign of a tech geek but of a well-run business, no matter how small. Like so many technological innovations, it is no longer a tech product but a business product.

**C** *a s e* **S** *t u d y*

## THE 21ST CENTURY COMES
## TO PHILADELPHIA

---

## PART I: BUYING IT ALL

Edmund Sterne, CPA/PFS, is realizing his dream. After doing time in the personal financial planning department of a national accounting firm, a two-partner accounting firm in Philadelphia has hired him to start a financial planning practice to augment their tax practice. Both partners are in their early 60s and have told Edmund that as they transition out of the business and into retirement, a partnership is a strong possibility.

The partners, Abigail and Mark, have an office manager, Sylvia, who handles all the appointments, takes care of billing and filing, and takes care of the myriad details of running a practice. She sent some 20 years of client records into a long-term storage facility to turn a storeroom into an office for Edmund. After he settled in, Abigail and Mark took Edmund out to lunch.

"I suppose," says Abigail, "that you have some idea of what kind of planning software you want to run." Agrees Mark, "Yes. We don't know much about financial planning software. It's pretty much up to you. Just keep us in the loop regarding the cost."

In fact, he continues, they want Edmund to become the de facto technology director for the firm. "The three of us—and now you—are all using different machines, and they're not networked," says partner one. "We still have dial-up Internet service. We need to upgrade a whole host of applications and can't because our machines don't have enough power—they're too old. We didn't even bother buying you a machine—I got my son a new laptop when he started college and gave you his old desktop system, temporarily." (Which explains, thinks Edmund, why the hard disk is almost completely filled with video games.)

"Can you get us properly set up for the 21st century?" asks Abigail.

Edmund thinks it over. "I can buy the right machines and software, and although I can't do the actual networking work, I can find the right vendors to help us set it up and give us ongoing maintenance. I can even get us training."

Mark signals the waiter for the check. "Great. Get started this afternoon."

Back in the office, Edmund goes online (slowly) long enough to download and print Walt Mossberg's most recent column from *The Wall Street Journal* on how to buy a computer. Then it's off to the ComputerWorld superstore just a few blocks away.

ComputerWorld has a full display of HP and Compaq computers lined up on long benches, ranked from least to most sophisticated. Although Edmund knows he could order a computer online through Dell, he likes to see exactly what he's getting. Also, he thinks he can get a volume discount on products and services if he buys locally.

Flagging down a sales associate, Edmund asks what each computer has that another model, costing $150 less, doesn't have. "Well, this one only has 128K RAM. That's the bare minimum for the latest Windows version, XP." Edmund knows that Windows XP runs best on 256K, and even better on 512K. Stopping at the second-to-most expensive model, Edmund says, "This model will run XP easily, play DVD disks, and both play and create CDs for record storage and client presentations. What do I get with the next model—and another $150?" For that, the associate says, you can create, or burn, DVDs as well as CDs. "Why would I want to do that?" asks Edmund. "If you make or edit digital movies," is the reply.

Film production is not a niche at his firm, so Edmund says he doesn't want this option. If burning DVDs becomes important later, for whatever reason, he knows that he can buy the feature as an add-on.

However, Edmund makes sure each machine has several Universal Serial Bus (USB) ports. These narrow "outlets" in the machine easily connect the latest mouse devices, PDAs, and other peripherals. They also have a built-in Ethernet card that will allow each machine to work with a high-speed Internet connection.

Edmund negotiates a discount for buying four identical machines, then moves on to monitors. "Look at these large, flat-screen monitors," says the associate. "Each comes with a $50 rebate. And they're not only sharp and clear, they'll take up virtually no room on your desk." Edmund orders four.

Next, he's ready to order a printer. The office currently has one large, creaky laser printer and a couple of dot matrix printers. Although dot matrix printers are fast, the print quality is poor, and they're incredibly loud. Edmund figures the firm could get a charitable deduction by donating them to the Smithsonian.

The office doesn't do a lot of printing, so Edmund figures the firm can get by with one new laser printer. The new models are relatively small and fast and simultaneously hold multiple kinds of paper—such as regular paper, stationery, and legal-size paper. A network will allow all of the users to share one printer and queue up their jobs. The office manager has more printing needs than anyone, but a lot of what she does is for internal use only—clients don't see it. So Edmund buys for her desk a small inkjet printer that can also print in color. It's quiet and almost as good as a laser printer.

His final hardware purchase is a scanner. He knows that the firm isn't ready to move into a paperless universe, and he knows he better not push his new bosses too far too fast. So he buys a low-end model for about $100 that includes OCR software, so it will read and recognize the text documents that are scanned in.

"Now," says Edmund, "do you have someone who can create a network for us? We have client files that four people may need to access from their own machines. We all want to use the same printer. If the laser printer is tied up printing a long proposal, and we just want to quickly print a couple of pages of directions from MapQuest, we want to be able to switch instantly to the color printer on the office manager's desk."

No problem. ComputerWorld is committed to their small business customers and has trained staff members who can install the machines and set up a local area network, or LAN, that connects them. Even more importantly, the LAN is expandable. If the business grows, the firm can easily add more computers and more printers. As he rings up the hardware purchases, the associate introduces Edmund to the service manager, who explains the costs and arranges someone to set it all up upon delivery.

"By the way," says the service manager, "you probably know that these computers come with several games already loaded. However, many of our business customers ask us to remove them before delivery to keep employees focused on their work. We will delete these for you at no extra charge." Edmund thinks about this. "Does it come with solitaire?" he asks. "That's standard," says the manager. "Then you can leave them on."

Edmund is also concerned about transferring everyone's files from the old machines to the new ones. The service manager says he can arrange a direct cable transfer from the old system to the new one with a special, one-time back-up utility. This reminds Edmund he's going to have to lecture his colleagues about backing up files onto CDs—perhaps that could be part of Sylvia's job. He's also going to look into a contract with Xdrive or Iron Mountain, companies that can do automatic offsite backups of entire systems.

Edmund's next job is to get everyone online. Currently, the company has dial-up service with AOL. He knows that, while this service has done a great job of getting millions of individuals started on the Internet, it is not nearly robust enough for heavy business use. Unfortunately, the office building is not wired for cable, and the local cable provider doesn't yet provide Internet service in their area anyway. However, Verizon provides high-speed DSL service that is available in their area. He calls the phone company and gets that set up.

Edmund tells the firm's partners the firm is going to be on the technological cutting edge. Mark looks at the invoices. "At these prices, I sure hope so," he says.

## PART II: MOVING TO ADVANCED TOPICS

It's now several weeks later, and Edmund's technology is all in place. The computers are set up, and everyone enjoys the ease of printing and the quick online access. The time savings are enough to offset the additional costs—looking up regulations and investment information online, which previously had to be found by looking through books and periodicals, is already saving hours. (Mark has stopped grumbling about the price.) Edmund has picked out and loaded the financial planning packages he wanted and is already meeting with clients. However, not everyone in the firm is getting the full benefit.

For example, over the years, Mark and Abigail have done various seminars for business groups around town. They have raised the firm's profile, which has led to new clients. They've asked some of these groups to let Edmund give a presentation on key financial planning topics.

"Great," says Edmund, "I'll pull together a nice PowerPoint presentation for them."

"Oh yeah. We've heard about PowerPoint, but we never used it," says Abigail. "We used some overheads, but when they got out of date, it became too much of a hassle to update them. We print out some Word and Excel material, photocopy it, and hand it out."

Edmund shows them what they were missing. "Look! I can embed an Excel sheet. I scanned in the firm logo from a piece of stationery and added it to each slide. And it's all in color. I'm waiting until the last minute to add the latest market figures for the Center City Business Owners's Association meeting. These may change radically by the time I'm ready to do my session at the local FPA meeting, but it takes me about five minutes to update them."

The partners are jealous. "Teach us to do this!" Sylvia, who has been looking over their shoulders at the demo, also looks interested. Now, Edmund has client meetings all day plus his own presentations to do. "I have a better idea. I can arrange for some low-cost training—and we should all attend." If Sylvia can learn PowerPoint, he explains, she can help create and update their presentations. She has had more time for these tasks since their more sophisticated tech set-up has saved her time on other tasks.

The Yellow Pages lists a number of training companies. Also, Sylvia, who is interested in expanding her skills, says she has a computer-whiz friend who works part-time and would be interested in offering PowerPoint training on a freelance basis.

"Does your friend also know Outlook?" asks Edmund. "In addition to being a great e-mail program, it also can keep track of our appointments. You know, with the firm growing, it's getting harder to keep track of where we all are. If we all entered our appointments on the computer, you would know where we were and when we were free." Warming to his subject, he continues, "And if we all had PDAs—you know, Palm Pilots—we would have all our appointments downloaded and could take them with us anywhere."

"I'm willing to try the central appointments system," says Mark. "But I've been using the same personal leather diary for 15 years, and I'm not sure I want to change right now." Edmund, who has just bought a color Palm for his own use, doesn't push the issue.

The impromptu meeting ends. Sylvia calls her friend. Edmund goes back to his office and shuts the door. He calls a number a friend at the local FPA chapter gave him. "Hi! I got your name from someone at DeSylva, Brown, and Henderson. He said you did his Web site. Could you give me some ballpark figures on what it would take to set up one for us . . ."

---

## EXECUTIVE SUMMARY

- Technology education is a continuous learning process.
- The proper technology set-up requires a late-model desktop, big screen, Microsoft programs, laser printer, and back-up system.
- One way or another, get a high-speed Internet connection; dial-up connections are too slow.

- Research local consultants and vendors to help you with your set-up.
- Use affiliated companies—custodians and broker-dealers—as resources.
- If you get bigger, then in-house, tech-savvy employees are a lifesaver. Experts are great, but even a curious, interested layperson can help a lot.
- Get yourself a PDA and related software to save time and money.
- Consider other time savers, such as voice recognition software and specialized e-mail services.
- For advanced users willing to work more closely with compliance experts, a completely paperfree office is possible and, ultimately, will lead to cost savings.
- Asset management software remains a difficult choice, but spend time finding what's best for you, without getting sucked into the politics of the day.
- You must have a Web site, and you need a professional to set it up for you.
- A Web site can help brand your firm and let you reach out to clients.

# 3

# KNOW THYSELF

have a friend who's a physi-
cian, and I remember that when he was in medical school, we
talked about what he wanted to specialize in. "It's a hard
choice. I'm interested in everything I study. Recently, I've really
been fascinated by surgery. But there's one major drawback."

"The sight of blood?" I asked.

"No. Having to spend time with other surgeons."

It's a funny story, but there's some truth there, too. You
have to consider all the aspects of your career choice, not just
the immediate job. My friend, a top student with a friendly,
down-to-earth manner, was only half kidding when he said he
didn't want to spend his career with a group that he saw as more
concerned with the patient as a problem to solve, rather than
as a person. He became a pediatrician and never regretted it.

Your practice model and the clients you go after are two
choices that affect each other. The industry argument of fees
versus commissions has many angles, most of them beyond the
scope of this book, but you do have to make a decision that

works with your ideal clientele. Although some wealthy individuals work with commission-based planners, they tend mostly to go to advisors who are mostly or entirely fee-based.

Of course, some advisors who get most or all of their income from fees can also work with middle-income clients, but they have to vary the traditional assets-under-management model. If someone has $10,000 to invest, are you going to charge 1 to 2 percent, that is, $100 to $200? This is less than what a top New York hairstylist can get at one appointment, and you're not getting a gratuity.

You'll also run into geographic constraints, even if you cast a wide net over more than one state. Don't specialize in technology executives if you live in Boise, Idaho, and don't wait for farmers to fill your office in Brooklyn.

Okay, that was obvious, but you can be a lot more subtle. For example, Amy Leavitt had heard that Vermont was well populated with small business owners. "I bought a list from Dun & Bradstreet with a list of all the businesses that were within a 90-minute radius of my office and that had at least 25 employees. I narrowed it with certain codes, because I wanted heavily capitalized business, such as contractors and manufacturers. I got something over 1,000 names, and I knew that that was going to be my career."

To get started, you can use the U.S. Census Bureau, which has a lot of free information online. For example, you can find out that in Rockland County, New York, where I live, the median household income is nearly $68,000, and 28 percent of the residents are under 18. That tells you there are lots of families, with good incomes. North and west of us is Orange County, which has nearly the same percentage of children—but a median income of only $52,000. Also, if you look at the transportation network, you will see that Rockland has a number of commuting options to New York City. Orange does not—residents tend to work locally. So you're going to find a different clientele.

That's just a small sample. A huge wealth of data is available, and because your tax dollars paid for it, you might as well use it.

## LOOKING AT INCOME

In an oft-told tale, the notorious bank robber, Willie Sutton, was asked why he robbed banks. "Because that's where they keep the money," he said.

Many planners have the same idea about high net-worth clients, that they hold all the money and, therefore, are the most desirable clients, and perhaps the only clients, worth courting. The media has to take some of the blame for this—whenever we quote a planner in an article, we usually try to get an assets-under-management number. David Yeske, who has served as president of the Financial Planning Association, has written that this number is "like rating your child's music teacher on the basis of how many pianos he or she has purchased."

The late *Worth* magazine came out with an annual list of the top financial planners, and although many terrific planners deserved to be there (some of whom are quoted in these pages), the list was heavily skewed to planners who serve wealthy clients. Not many small-town planners, who help middle-income clients balance their 401(k) plans, put a few dollars into a 529 plan, and buy the right life insurance, made it.

Yet, don't forget the surgeon story. Many planners have found considerable personal satisfaction in serving the middle market. Then, if that's not enough incentive for you, these planners have also found enviable economic success.

Most planners are going to have to start small, anyway. Especially if you're new to the profession and relatively young, few people are going to want to hand you a multimillion dollar portfolio to handle.

Deena Katz said, "You can't start out and say, 'I'm going to charge $10,000 a year! Everybody has to have $1 million to work with me!' You're going to be pretty hungry. Most people can't just start with high net-worth individuals. You generally don't run in those circles. If you're young, no one is interested in what you have to say."

Katz started in real estate management and had access to wealthy individuals before she became a full-fledged financial planner. If you're a CPA with a history of preparing tax returns for the wealthy, that also gives you an entree. The same is true for certain lawyers, who may have done trust or estate planning work. But most have to start from scratch.

Even if you eventually move to wealthy individuals on a fee-only basis, "you have to build toward that," said Katz. "In the beginning, you'll be doing some commission work, because people at lower income levels will want to pay you differently than the high net-worth clients. They're the ones who are comfortable with fees and can afford to pay you." Like many firms, Katz's has minimums, and they often rise over time. "We've moved up our minimums over time. But it takes a mature practice."

## CHOOSING—AND CHARGING—CLIENTS

John Bowen focuses on helping advisors reach the high net-worth market. "First, see if the market can support you," he advises. "Where is the money? Is there a high concentration of wealth in your area? Are they being served?" Most planners have not gone through this process. Finding the right clients has been happenstance, said Bowen, and that can be a dangerous way to build your practice. "You have to identify your ideal client, or you're setting yourself up to have mediocre success. You can't serve everyone. This is Business 101."

As Ed Slott says, "I think you have to pick some kind of area just to be great at. You can't be great at everything any more. There is just too much information out there. Planners make this mistake, so I tell them to pick something and be good at it:

divorce planning, whatever." He gets frustrated when he asks planners what they want to specialize in, and they say, "Well, I'm going to specialize in high net-worth clients." "Well, what is that?" he shoots back. "That's what everybody wants. That's not a specialty! I know so many firm descriptions read 'high net-worth.'"

That's why Slott picked IRAs—and the clients who relied on them for retirement. "I picked up on this IRA thing in the late 80s, when it was starting, and you *know* that is where all the money in America is and is going to be." There are millions of IRAs out there, and nobody seemed to know how to distribute the money. "I found it an unbelievable and powerful market to build my future on. In fact, I've bet my whole livelihood on it. And it has really paid off."

A targeted income level is an important consideration, but there are other issues—the age and occupations of clients, for example. Says Bowen: "If you're located in California, where I am, consider Silicon Valley. Even more specifically, consider midmarket employees of Hewlett-Packard. Ask yourself, 'Can I become an HP expert?' You can specialize in them through their human resources department, learn about their retirement plan. It can be easy if you think through it strategically."

Only a few of the planners I spoke with were very focused from the start. Others got what they could in the beginning and waited to see what developed as their practices matured. Some were even hard pressed to define their clients beyond saying that the clients had personality traits that meshed with their own— perhaps the most targeted list of all (and a successful one, too).

For example, Sharon Kayfetz said that perhaps the single common denominator for her clients was "how serious they were about improving their financial life. That's it. There are no minimums, no income floor." She also insisted on comprehensive planning—she didn't feel she could be a true planner just by handling a college planning engagement or helping with a rollover. She wanted complete involvement in her clients' financial lives.

Nancy Langdon Jones also had considerations more important than income level—even though, as with many planners, she didn't have much choice in the beginning. "About 20 years ago, anyone could be a client. But I realized I liked working with the middle-income client." As she once said in a magazine interview, "Rich people have the same problems as poor people— they're just busy making payments on their BMW instead of their Honda."

It turned out to be a good business decision. The high net-worth market may have been fully served in her area, but the middle market was very underserved. "The feeling is that they can't afford financial planning but need it just as much as anyone else. For them, even little mistakes that aren't very expensive in the scheme of things can be devastating. So they really do need help. I've tried to be a champion in that area."

Jones takes care of about 70 families. "You know, people told me there was no way I could make a living like this." She was told the only way anyone could make a living would be to have thousands of clients, giving each just minimal attention but selling lots of products. "How on earth could I keep track of that many! As it is now, I can see my clients walking down the street, and we know each other."

Morris Armstrong also grew and became increasingly successful, and although he's not entirely middle income, he manages to hold on to a range of clients within a small practice. "I have a lot of middle-income clients, and although I never consciously reached out to them, I have some high net-worth as well." He started as a commission-based planner and garnered his early clients among teachers by becoming active in the 403(b) market.

Like many planners, he eventually switched to a fee-only model, which is generally more popular with wealthier clients. But he also found that in the long term, people are more important than fidelity to a model. "A few teachers actually became clients when I moved to fee-only, even though they didn't have the balances, the account size, to warrant my services. But when someone has been with you for five years, you don't just drop them because you change your model." He charges the posted rates and imposes no minimum.

And, in trying to keep his old clients and get new ones, Armstrong has put his finger on one of the key issues in working with clients of your choice: how do you create a pricing structure that supports your business and keeps your clients happy? Armstrong solved the problem by offering multiple pricing structures. "I have an hourly fee. Then I have a flat fee for planning—deluxe plan and regular plan. The deluxe is mostly estate issues and so on, but few need it. If I manage money for clients, I have the assets-under-management fee. These clients also get access to my services included—they can ask questions throughout the year." There are no additional charges, unless clients want something complex, like an estate plan.

Mixed models also work for planners who get part of their income from commissions. Forward looking, independent broker-dealers, such as LPL, Raymond James, and Lincoln/Sagemark, increasingly are supporting fee-based reps. Amy Leavitt combined the best of both worlds, selling financial plans and then, if the client wanted, selling products to fulfill the plan. Why does this work so well? Leavitt points out that she is selling the value item, the plan, and taking away the emphasis on the product fulfillment, which is the commodity part. Too many planners get that backward, she says, seeing the plan as the giveaway and the product fulfillment as the money maker.

Although Armstrong is a member of NAPFA, and thus completely committed to a fee-only model for all his clients, it is possible to have some fee-only clients (usually at the high end) and some clients to whom you sell commission products and, for example, a financial plan for a flat or hourly fee.

Planner and tech guru John Olsen has a whole range of services with a corresponding whole range of clients, even though he has a one-person firm. Each one has its own compensation stream. He admits, with a laugh, that, "I have a very strange practice. It's actually in four parts. Financial and estate planning for retail customers. I'm also a life insurance agent." He sells insurance and related products, which may not have anything to do with financial planning. "If somebody wants a life insurance policy and doesn't need a comprehensive financial plan, I can do that." He also does a lot of consulting for other advisors. "That's a large part of my practice. I help them out in a particular area—I'm working on a big estate planning case right now. The planner called me in because we're dealing with some fairly abstruse stuff." Finally, he does software consulting, to both individuals and, now, to the actual manufacturers of software, helping them with development.

Other commission planners have also been successful in finding a solid niche—or multiple solid niches. Ric Edelman is perhaps unique in that he came into financial planning from journalism. Disgusted after covering an industry that seemed centered around tax shelters that enriched promoters at the expense of clients, he told himself, "Just look at all the money these guys are making giving bad advice. Imagine if I got into the business and actually tried to give good advice." Which he found himself eminently capable of doing.

Like Armstrong, Edelman began his career in schools, although instead of approaching teachers, he talked to parents about college planning. But, as his firm took off, he figured he could serve just about everyone by providing solid advice, if he had enough people. "The only way I can define our client base is that it is mass market. I don't think anyone has done what we've done. Every time I talk with other advisors about their practices, they're all pretty much targeting high net-worth individuals, or doctors, or business owners, or retirees, or some narrow demographic." Edelman's target? "People who want an education and want effective services in their best interests. And that cuts across all demographics."

By boldly trying to reach everyone and staffing up to do this, he's grasped a very broad crosssection of clients. Helping is his Washington, D.C., location, which includes some very affluent areas as well as some modest and positively poor neighborhoods. "Our poorest client owes $265,000 to credit cards. He makes $800,000 a year, so he doesn't care. It doesn't bother him nearly as much as it bothers us. His debt service is $14,000 a month. Obviously, he has no money with us—we just do debt counseling for him. On the other extreme, we've got a couple of clients who are dot-com billionaires. One client is among the wealthiest people in the Washington area. And we have everyone in between. Our average account size is $250,000. But we have a lot of clients who have nothing more than a $100 a month that they send us."

Even at his scale, however, Edelman is still subject to geographic realities, and he is sure to make use of it: a third of his clientele (like, probably, a third of Washington) is in the military or government.

Edelman says he is upset that some planners have account minimums. "You know, unless you have a half million, they won't talk to you. That's like a doctor saying, 'If you're sick, I won't help you.'" As you start your practice, think not only about which clients you want, but which clients need you. "The people who need our help the most are those with the least assets. Does a guy with a million really need your help? He already has the million! It's the guy who *wants* the million who needs your help."

Edelman has 18 planners working for him and a vast support staff—necessary to handle some 6,500 clients. But a large office is not the only way to branch out to the middle market.

## THE GARRETT MODEL

Sheryl Garrett found yet another way to reach a middle market, on a fee-only basis. It was one of those achievements everyone said couldn't be done. Conventional wisdom said that middle-income planning was incompatible with a fee-only model: The asset-under-management arrangement clearly would not work. Could you get an average salaried individual to pay an hourly fee or flat fee when he could go to a commissioned-based planner? Garrett thought so and was proved right—she now has 600 clients in a profitable practice. Yes, other fee-only planners had done this before Garrett, but she created a particularly powerful, new model that can serve as a template for other advisors who want to practice this way.

In fact, she created a network of other planners who want to do what she does—the Garrett Planning Network. She has nearly 160 planners in the network, and it continues to grow. Any planner interested in middle-market planning should look into it.

Garrett's move to middle income didn't just happen. It came out of a frustration with a former practice that was aimed at high-net-worth clients. "We'd get calls from people we couldn't help, and I didn't have anyone to refer them to." This seemed like an appalling gap to a planner who had herself grown up middle class.

From a business perspective, she didn't have to compete, because no one else was doing this. "Why establish a practice where you're destined to compete, if you could instead design a practice that your competitors will help build." That is, every high net-worth practice in the area, instead of becoming a competitor, became a source of referrals when they came across clients who didn't meet their minimums.

The Garrett model for serving middle-income clients is straight hourly planning or flat project-based fees. No asset-based fees. No annual retainer and no freebies, either. To make this model pay, every client pays for every minute. If a client calls just to ask a five-minute question about changing a portfolio mix, that's billable time.

But it's about more than middle-income planning. After all, if a wealthy client likes this model, neither Garrett nor anyone in her network is going to turn him or her away, and in fact, she does have some wealthy clients. However, she will turn away "delegators." She is only interested in "validators." Whether you ultimately join the Garrett network or not, this is another division in the kinds of clients you reach.

Delegators wants to turn over their entire financial life to you. This is the more traditional model—it's what wealthy clients especially crave, the ability to dump their financial lives into someone else's lap and get periodic reports. But, if you're a Garrett planner, you deal with validators. These people generally run their own financial lives but need some professional financial advice. This could be as little as coming in every year or so to rebalance a 401(k). Garrett will also write up a full financial plan. But she will not take over someone's entire financial situation.

Validation means relatively little commitment from the client. A traditional planner will likely require a transfer of assets and accounts, and even if there is no contractual commitment to remain with a planner long term, the complexities involved in joining a full service planner and subsequently leaving make many potential clients anxious. However, Garrett says she asks so little of her clients, they feel they have nothing to lose, and a lot to gain, by signing up for some hourly advice. Her closure rate is nearly 100 percent. *Hourly as-needed advice* is her motto.

The question you have to ask yourself is not, "Is this practice model viable?" It certainly is. Rather, it is, "Do I want to serve validators, or do I want a more delegator relationship?" It's a psychological decision, but it's also a business decision, because how you arrange and organize your pricing structure will change.

Consider how Jones charges, by way of comparison. She has multiple, fee-based models. Although she does have an hourly option, she also has some more delegator-friendly choices: a simple plan that can meet the needs of very modest clients, a comprehensive plan that includes management of assets up to $250,000, and a pure asset-under-management model.

Finally, Stephanie Parlee, CFP, in Old Town, Maine, doesn't have any clients at all. At least, no retail clients. In 2003, I invited her to participate in a planner roundtable we hosted at *Financial Planning* magazine, and she shared her interesting mode: "I do outsource planning for planners. I currently work with about three regular financial planners, doing their plans for them. And I'm looking at bringing in other outsourcers and working with another planner, so that hopefully that niche can be filled."

This was a lifestyle choice for her. This back office consulting system takes away the pressure of maintaining a traditional practice. "I have a two-year-old. I don't want a retail business. I'm good at planning and supporting other advisors. I was beating my head against the wall trying to make a go of the retail side, which isn't where my strengths are. So I did a lot of soul searching this last year and made the leap, and it's been great. I just love the numbers."

A good idea? One of the other participants started to explore hiring her during our discussion, and since then, several planners have called me for her phone number.

This is a lot of information, so I'm going to pause and give a pop quiz now.

Which is the best model for a planner?

1. High net-worth, asset-under-management model
2. Middle-income, hourly model
3. A variety of clients, a variety of models, within one practice
4. Selling advice plus commission products
5. All of the above, plus some others

The answer, of course is 5. Garrett, Jones, and others may have made their practice choices largely for emotional reasons—and there's no problem with that—but they ultimately based their practices on business decisions. They knew there was an

---

**FIGURE 3.1**  *Where Advisors Spend Their Time*

Are you doing what you want to be doing? As you form your practice, decide where your strengths are, figure out what you must do to create a successful practice, and choose what can be outsourced. This chart shows what advisors spend their time doing. Is this what you want to be doing? Different practitioners in this book change this mix so they are doing what they want to do, and others, inside or outside the firm, take responsibility for other slices. (Source: Moss Adams)

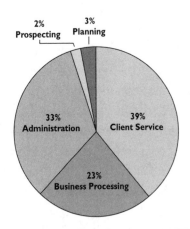

---

abundance of clients they wanted to reach in their area, and they knew they had to structure a business and pricing model that these clients would accept. (Figure 3.1 shows how planners are spending their time.)

## GIVE ME THAT OLD TIME MODEL

By now, I hope you realize that there's more to offering advice than just choosing rich versus middle-income clients and charging a fee or a commission. (If not, retake the pop quiz above.)

Of course, many will want to reach the high net-worth market, plain and simple, using the fee-only model with which these wealthy individuals are most comfortable. Actually, that's not quite correct. It's not plain and simple. Even top, midsized, fee-only firms reach different clients and operate in different ways.

In stressing the financial and emotional success that can come from working with middle-income clients, I didn't want to imply that those who work with high net-worth do so just for monetary reasons. There is emotional satisfaction, and special challenges, with this group. One planner I spoke with told of an extremely wealthy client who called him late at night, at home. His client had just met his daughter's fiancé, and wanted to know, at 11:00 PM, what the advisor was going to do to keep the family money out of the hands of this "fortune hunter."

When considering working with high net-worth clients, however, keep in mind that this is a catch-all term, not a segment you can just go after. The wealthy, depending on where and how the money was acquired, have different ideas about how it should be managed. Don't think you can aim at the entire wealthy spectrum. You have to look at what kind of high net-worth clients you want. In New York City, a millionaire is likely someone who has made his money on Wall Street or who is a top surgeon. In Nebraska, it might be someone who inherited a business or built up an inherited business and lives in a house built by his grandfather.

The psychological difference can be enormous. I chatted at a conference with a planner in Michigan who had some high net-worth clients. Some of them insisted on keeping substantial assets in local, Rust Belt industries. He had often strenuously advised greater diversification. "But they felt a strong loyalty to the region and economy."

Consider Dan Moisand—his typical clients are millionaires or close to it, "but not multimillionaires," he says. "Someone once gave me a piece of advice: review your clients from the perspective of whom you most enjoy working with, not necessarily those who provide the most revenue." If you pull a file at random from his cabinet, says Moisand, "You'll probably find someone who is retired or close to it. And probably someone who has been happily married for many years—although why that is, I have no idea!" They're also, he said, people who have money because they saved or, possibly, have family money. "I enjoy working with them."

As we'll see in greater detail in the chapters on marketing and public relations, what clients you get and how you go about getting them are tightly connected. Your first clients, having had a good experience with you, will likely tell their friends, who likely as not, will be people like them. A 60-year-old couple will probably have other 60-year-old couple friends. "They tell two people, who tell two people, that kind of thing—and so on," says Moisand. Your practice can change as it grows, but if it grows heavily by referrals—a good thing—you may find new clients bear a strong resemblance to earlier ones.

One planner found herself with about half a dozen chiropractors, after an early chiropractor client recommended her to friends and colleagues he knew from a professional organization.

If you have a practice in Silicon Valley, you might have tech millionaires. If you're in Manhattan, it's probably Wall Street millionaires. But if you're in Pittsburgh, like Lou Stanasolovich, you're in a county with one of the oldest median ages in the country, which accounts for the fact that about 85 percent of Stanasolovich's clients are over 50, and 30 percent are over 65. A problem? "No, this is an advantage for us. We don't have megamillionaires, like you might have in Atlanta or San Francisco. We don't have that kind of client all that often. But we have quite a few people who have saved and who are millionaires." Altogether, he has about 160 clients.

Doctors account for about 40 percent of his practice. But he's also reaching out to business owners, a growing segment. "We've always been real strong on doctors." Despite complaints that HMOs are playing havoc with physician income, Stanasolovich said it is still a high-earning profession. And, like Moisand with his group, once he got known among them, referrals brought in more. "I had always focused on doctors. It's still a higher-earning profession, and we end up getting known among those people."

Ross Levin, just outside of Minneapolis, is heavily involved with physicians, inherited wealth, and executives, as well as a number of retirees. He assembled this group over time as he raised his fees, thus gradually focusing on wealthier and wealthier clients. He started with a minimum fee of $1,000 a year. Now it's up to $10,000. He has about 200 clients.

"We've identified the type of clients we like to work with. They're delegators." Think about it—if you're writing a check for $10,000, you expect your advisor to take care of your life. "Our clients value advice and are willing to pay for it. They view us as their first call for questions. We do everything for our clients. We refinance their mortgages. We buy them cars. We do all that kind of stuff. We like working with physicians and inherited wealth, because they are two groups that have similar values to ours." Again, beyond the money, the psychological and emotional issues remain key. You must structure your business to work with these. "We can get much deeper than just the money aspects—we can get into what our clients want to do with your life."

As noted consultant Bill Bachrach says, "Focus on the right kind of client from the beginning and learn all about that kind of client, and really just service them to the nth degree so they don't need any other advisor."

## SO, MORE CLIENTS = MORE MONEY?

Well, yes, but how many clients can you handle? Edelman, as noted above, handles some 6,500 clients but with 18 other planners, who are free to do nothing but planning because of the huge support staff. It's a manageable number. Other planners in practices with multiple professionals can also handle more clients than sole practitioners, even though the planner-client ratio may be similar. (See Chapter 5, "Master of the House," for more on this.)

What's a manageable number for you? Assuming you are a comprehensive planner working with delegators, the wealthier your clients, the more you will earn from them. But, because their financial situations tend to be more complex than those involving less money, you will not be able to handle as many of them.

Right after exhorting planners to serve clients fully, Bachrach says, "You can't be a comprehensive planner and a trusted advisor to 700 people. It isn't physically possible. I spoke to a client recently who has realized he only needs 20 clients. When I started coaching him, he was going to have 100 clients. Five months into it, he thought that 100 clients would be a big reduction. But now he realizes he just needs 20. They're high net-worth—with a minimum of $10 million in investable assets each." Now, Bachrach admits that people with that much money are not just floating around, but he said the advisor discovered, "It would take him less time to get 20 high net-worth clients than it would take to get 100 middle income clients."

Twenty may be an unusually small number, but it illustrated Bachrach's point that you need to get a core group you can effectively work with. "Most trusted advisors we work with end up with 75 to 150 clients, whose assets run in the $200,000 to $1 million range."

Of course, you have to do the math—how much are you charging each of your 100 clients, for example? Does that yield a suitable income for you? (Make yourself your own first client!) But whatever niche you find, don't overextend yourself. You may end up with hundreds of clients, but you won't be able to keep all, or even most, of them happy and loyal.

Says Bachrach, "Every client is going to have a comprehensive plan, and you'll manage *all* of their assets, be their full-service advisor, helping them with assets and insurance and other topics. You can't do that for 600 to 800 people, or even more."

Bachrach quotes his Being Done Mantra—Being Done: "I have 150 loyal clients who happily pay me $5,000 minimum per year to be their Trusted Advisor. They all have written plans and they follow my advice. My phone hardly rings, regardless of what's happening in the market. I don't prospect any more. I just serve my clients." Your numbers may be different, says Bachrach, but you get the point.

## ANSWER THE BIG QUESTION

I keep skirting around the question, but it's only fair to address it: which is better, fees or commissions? This question has led to intense debate involving the CFP Board of Standards, the Financial Planning Association, and the National Association of Personal Financial Advisors (NAPFA), the organization of fee-only planners. It is not going to be resolved any time soon. In fact, I revisit this issue in Chapter 7, "Doing Well by Doing Good," in the context of ethics and whether you come across to prospective clients.

For the purposes of this book, however, you should know that fees are becoming more a part of financial planning. Relatively few true financial planners work entirely on commission. Planners who are registered reps increasingly charge separately for assembling a plan—Amy Leavitt is a key example of this. Some planners work on commission with some clients (usually middle-income) and just for fees with others (usually wealthy).

A fee-based practice will likely prove more stable in the long run, but it's harder to get started. Many planners begin as a registered rep, selling on commission, while doing true planning with a Certified Financial Planner or some other well-known designation. No matter what your clientele, you may be able to move more to fees. However, if this payment system upsets some clients, be aware that you may lose them and consider whether you can replace them. Morris Armstrong found a way to keep his old clients even as he moved into new areas, and you may find this approach best for practical and ethical reasons.

The good news is that broker-dealers are becoming increasingly anxious about losing great planners because they have moved to fee-only and have no need for a broker-dealer affiliation. They are generally making it easier for reps to create a fee-based or even a fee-only practice and retain the affiliation under another arrangement. If you think you might head in that direction, ask your broker-dealer about their policy.

The financial planning profession is still young, and there's an explosion in the methods of practicing and ways of reaching out to different niches and different income levels. You can develop ways of structuring your practice to reach the clients you want to reach with a compensation method they find acceptable.

C a s e  S t u d y

## PLACES IN THE HEART

Katie Spenser has worked as an employee agent for a large, regional broker-dealer for years in Boston. She has been increasingly successful, earning higher and higher commissions. However, she has been feeling some personal and professional dissatisfaction. She is tired of life in the big city and spends more and more time wishing she could be at her vacation home in Pleasanton, in rural Massachusetts. At the same time, she is less interested in her clientele—a rather homogenous mix of urban, high net-worth clients. Although Katie has her CFP designation, she doesn't get to do much true planning, thanks to her firm's strong emphasis on sales—a transactional rather than consultative process. She has the necessary Series licenses and various state insurance licenses as well.

Katie wonders if she can make a living in Pleasanton with a different atmosphere and a different kind of clientele. *Financial Planning* magazine profiles in detail the top 50 or so independent broker-dealers—how big they are, the kinds of products the reps sell, and payouts. She closets herself in her office on a slow day and starts making phone calls.

Eventually, after some weeks of discussion and consideration, she finds an independent broker-dealer—Acme Financial—that would be happy to take her on and see her established in Pleasanton. But can she make a living there? Even though, at Acme, she isn't going to have the pressure to produce that she had at her regional firm, she is still going to have to meet minimums. These minimums are not only to remain affiliated with Acme but to pay her mortgage, set up her office, and eat three meals a day.

The first place for her to go is to the Census Bureau Web site <www.census.gov>, where she can quickly view the economic makeup of Pleasant County—the area surrounding Pleasanton. She goes to the State and County Quick Facts section, which profiles each county in the country, as well as the Economic Census section, which has detailed business information.

She finds that Pleasanton traditionally has had an agrarian economy, but this has faded over the years. The old family farms have pretty much disappeared as their elderly owners have retired and died and their heirs sold the land to developers eager to build weekend homes for well-to-do Boston residents—like Katie herself. It's getting harder and harder to find the farm-fresh tomatoes and corn that she brings back with her to Boston on Sunday nights.

At first glance, this profile is not a promising one for Katie's practice. The weekend residents are likely to have financial advisors who can serve them in Boston. But a closer reading of the data shows that more and more people are settling more or less permanently in Pleasant County as they retire. Katie feels confident that she can succeed by providing them immediate, local service regarding estate planning and retirement issues. The average income of a county resident has risen faster in recent years than that of the state as a whole.

Who else is there? She invests in some reports from Dun & Bradstreet and even pores over the county Yellow Pages book.

Attracted by the low taxes and good schools, professionals and small business owners who can afford to be that far from a major city have relocated to Pleasanton. (Good schools? Maybe the teachers need help with their 403(b) plans.) There's a small commercial printer at the edge of town, for example. The building boom has supported contractors, carpenters, and plumbers. The influx of retirees has encouraged the growth of better restaurants, and next year, the hospital's new wing will be completed. More doctors and nurses will be joining.

Katie wonders if she can knit a practice out of all of these demographics, and thinks she can. She divides her potential clients into four categories: high net-worth retirees; local business owners; doctors and other hospital employees, especially executives; and teachers. The trouble is, they'll have radically different needs and will relate to the concept of financial advice differently. The retirees will have extensive funds in IRAs, 401(k) plans, and other vehicles. Some of them will have portfolios that were started by their grandparents and great-grandparents. Katie will need to focus on the best ways to access that money and help them make it last for the rest of their lives. Indeed, these clients will expect to leave a sizable inheritance to their children and grandchildren.

The business owners are concerned with the intersection between personal and company concerns. If they're relatively young, they want to know how to start savings plans for themselves and their employees. They'll want Katie to help them set up SEPs and SIMPLEs—are they big enough to have a 401(k)? Older ones are concerned with transition issues, such as properly dividing the business among their children, only some of whom may be actively involved. On the other hand, if none of the children is interested in the business, but several long-time employees are, Katie will need to help them plan and perhaps even finance an employee buyout.

The doctors have particular problems, as many of them could be on a path to a high net-worth career, even while they struggle in the beginning with huge student loans and down payments on homes.

Finally, the teachers are in a stable profession. The influx of business owners and others has led to an increase of school-aged children in the county after years of gradual decline. However, teachers will never make huge salaries. Their needs will be for help in the management of retirement plans, learning about various insurance products, and advice on 529 plans to help their own kids afford college.

Not only will Katie need to master a wide-ranging skill set, she'll also need to adjust her compensation model. Fortunately, Acme Financial allows, and even encourages, its financial planner reps to mix fee and commission compensation models within one practice. If the model passes regulatory muster and keeps the client happy, it's okay with Acme. The teachers, Katie believes, won't be comfortable laying out a lot of money. She believes she can assemble a simple, low-cost financial plan that includes 403(b) advice and sell the necessary insurance products on commission. (The market could be even bigger if she can become an official 403(b) provider at the school.)

The retirees, on the other hand, could be quite well-off and may be used to a fee-only model. Some of them may have solid portfolios that need little adjustment but may want to come in occasionally for adjustments and one-time help with legacy issues. She may be able to charge them on retainer or by the hour. For the business owners, it could be a mix. For example, the young couple who just opened a deli (fellow urban refugees secretly expecting a Norman Rockwell world) have little capital but need advice. They might be happiest, like the teachers, with a plan—sold at a fee—that is implemented with commission products. Older owners with successful, mature businesses may be happiest with a retainer as Katie addresses their legacy issues.

The doctors may be a good candidate for more comprehensive services. They're exceptionally busy but will have a gradually, or even rapidly, growing portfolio. The traditional asset-under-management model might suit them well.

Katie considers her options. Although she hopes to expand her office in the future, right now she is just running a one-person office and has a limited amount of time. Even if she had a magic wand to instantly attract new clients in all these different niches, does she really have time to serve them all as they deserve? That is, if she lands wealthy retirees, they'll expect her to keep up with the latest options and regulations surrounding trusts and estate taxes. The teachers will want someone who is an expert on the particular fund options with their 403(b) plan. She'll have to exhaustively research each fund.

What about the business owners? She'll need to keep up on all the SEP and SIMPLE regulations. Also, does she really want to involve herself again with the demanding, high net-worth clients, like doctors, laboriously getting them into separately managed accounts and explaining why they lost a percentage point last quarter?

Why did she consider moving to Pleasanton in the first place?

It wasn't to become extraordinarily wealthy. If that's what she wanted, she tells herself, she would stay in Boston. She wants to change her life and support herself comfortably in a town and county she's grown to love.

Forgetting the business end for a moment, Katie realizes that two groups will give her the greatest personal satisfaction: the small business owners and the teachers. After all, her father was a high school math teacher, and when she was growing up, her house was full of her father's teacher friends. She likes them and understands them. As for the small business owners—she is one herself. Katie makes a commitment to offer these groups comprehensive financial planning but to specialize in the retirement and transition issues so important to both groups. She plans to create a series of easy-to-customize template plans that will allow her to serve both groups economically and still make a profit.

If she happens to land any wealthy retirees or physicians, or if one of her small business clients gets incredibly successful and needs more intensive portfolio management services than she can provide, she knows colleagues from the FPA who don't have a retail practice but just provide portfolio services to other advisors on an outsourcing basis.

Pleased with her decision, Katie dashes a note off to her landlord, telling him that she won't be renewing her lease on her apartment, and she wonders if she will get enough for her Mercedes to buy a brand new four-wheel drive Suburu.

---

## EXECUTIVE SUMMARY

- Practice models and desired clients are two choices that are closely related.
- You can practice for fees, commissions, or a mix, but even within each choice, there are dozens of variations.
- You can focus on certain clients by becoming an expert.
- The kinds of clients you can get will be based heavily on geography.
- Don't get hung up thinking that high net-worth is the only way to go—you can be very successful with middle-income clients.
- If you do work with wealthy clients, there are still differences among various subgroups.
- Many planners work heavily with specific age levels or professions.
- You should consider whether you want to handle validators or delegators.
- Do some math—how many clients can you truly handle, and what will your ultimate income be?
- Fee vs. commission remains a controversial issue, but you need to pick what works for you and your clients.

# 4

# SELL YOURSELF

I once worked at a publication where, every time we had a lunch event such as taking out a new employee, we invariably ended up at a Chinese restaurant. We always got fortune cookies, and I'd pin the fortunes onto my bulletin board when I got back to the office. My favorite one, which I still carry in my wallet, was, "A wise man knows everything. A shrewd man knows everyone."

In this chapter, you will learn how to become shrewd.

Marketing, sales, public relations—these are the exposure aspects of your practice, the tasks that require you to leave your desk and become seen and heard. You may despise these tasks, but you're going to have to get good at them, and you're probably better at them than you think. If you are comfortable sitting with a client and talking about their financial problems, you will probably be comfortable talking in other venues as well.

In fact, you may surprise yourself. Some planners I know became so good at being rainmakers and spokespersons, they began spending more and more time boosting the business, joining with other planners, and hiring staff to handle the day-to-day management of the firm.

Don't make the mistake of thinking there is only one way to approach marketing and public relations—or that a huge financial outlay is necessary. There is more than one way of reaching out effectively, and although some methods can get expensive, many are low-budget, especially suitable for new planners.

For example, I knew an accountant with a tax practice in a small town. In the days when those who did their own returns used pen and paper, he bought bottles of correction fluid and put his own labels on them: "If you're doing your own taxes, you'll need this." He also dug through the Internal Revenue Code for some of the most complex and confusing regulatory language (he didn't have to look long). He then copied the paragraphs onto a flyer with the caption: "If you understand this, you should prepare your own taxes. Otherwise, you should contact me."

I'm discussing three different topics here, but they're all related:

1. *Marketing.* Marketing means promoting your firm through multiple means, using free and paid channels.
2. *Advertising.* Advertising means taking paid notices in newspapers, using direct mail, buying radio commercials, etc., to obtain new clients.
3. *Public relations.* Public relations means creating a widespread, positive image for your firm.

You could make a distinction among these, but I think they're better understood as part of a bigger picture—*getting noticed.* Sometimes the effect is direct and immediate: you hold a seminar and, ideally, a number of participants call you the next day to establish a relationship. Sometimes the connection is less direct, although no less important. If you get quoted in influential and respected publications, no one may call you the next

day just because they saw your name in the local newspaper—
or even in *Money* or *The Wall Street Journal,* but the quotes will
build your business in the long run.

I've created what I like to think of as an Awareness List.
This is not arranged as best to worst or inexpensive to costly.
Rather, it's from simple to sophisticated.

**The Awareness List**

- Referrals
- Advertising
- Seminars
- Getting quoted / press releases
- Writing
- Speaking at conferences

This is not an either/or list. You don't have to give up one
item to move to the next. In fact, you shouldn't. It is a progres-
sively complex list. That is, as you go down the list, your techniques for mastering that item will have to be more subtle, more
refined. We're going to take them step by step.

# REFERRALS
## Meeting Friends, and Friends of Friends

This method is the most basic for getting known, and it's
the most essential. If you can't count on current clients to recommend you, nothing else will work. I have never met a successful planner who didn't rely heavily on references, especially
when building a practice. Often, in a mature practice, the planner has all the clients they can handle but still gets referrals
without trying. (If the referral is a close friend or a relation of
a current client whom you don't want to disappoint, you do
your best to squeeze them in.)

What's great about referrals is that you can get them from the day you open your practice. The best illustration comes from Bill Bachrach. This is only a part of his extraordinary, values-based system.

So you're just starting out, says Bachrach, and you say, "I'm brand new—I have no clients! What do I do?" Traditionally, planners came out of a heavy sales environment in a wirehouse or insurance company, for example, and are unused to the different atmosphere in a consulting-based, financial planning practice.

Bachrach has developed a proprietary road map system (Financial Road Map), which helps you gain new clients and provide great service based on your clients' attitudes about money. He teaches it and then urges you to practice it, even before you have a viable practice. "Call up everyone you know, every friend and relative, and say, 'I'm new to the financial services biz, and I have a really cool process, and whether we ever do business or not, you'll get value from the process. We're going to do your Financial Road Map, and you'll get a chance to experience my new career. And I really need to practice. Would you help me out?'"

About half the time, more or less, says Bachrach, the person with whom you are doing your practice session will turn to you at the end say, "Okay, what happens next?" Your response would be, "Well, if you wanted to hire me, if this were for real, the next step would be to put together a plan for you. I have all these resources. I know I'm brand new, but the money managers I work with have been in the biz for a billion years. I work at this great company. We have great resources. So I'm taking this info back to my company to come back with an action plan—specifically for you so you will achieve your goals and fulfill what is truly important to you (your values).

Some of these "practice clients" end up saying, "Well, I'd like to do that," and you say, "Well, that wasn't our deal—I don't want you to think I was doing a big switch on you here." You honor the deal, says Bachrach, but if you do his system right, he says, people will go, "Wow, I've been with same broker for 17 years, and he doesn't know what's really important to me (my core values). He doesn't know my goals, and you got me more clarity in a half-hour practice session then my advisor has in 17 years."

So, even if you have clients, this is a low-pressure way to start gathering clients. What's great is that it is nonthreatening to these practice clients. It couldn't be more different from a traditional sales approach. Have you ever had a friend contact you just to sell you some insurance? Did you like it? The Bachrach system is about consulting, not selling. I'm not doing full justice to the Bachrach values-based system, but new and growing planners especially should check out his books, videos, and seminars.

John Bowen, who has reviewed many studies and whose firm has released more than a few itself, says that nothing beats a good referral network.

Although the power of referrals seems self-evident, several angles can help you get the maximum value out of them. Business consultant Michael Lovas advises planners not to overlook any possible source—even a client who isn't a top source of income can be a top source of referrals. "If I spend time working with Joe and Mary-Anne, and they only buy a little annuity from me—well, I didn't make as much money. But maybe I connected with a family who will bring me a bunch of referrals. And by treating them with respect, I invite them to refer people to me. I become magnetic."

Ross Levin urges planners to consider the mathematics of referrals. "Our philosophy has been that, if we like a client, there's a high probability that they've got friends who will be similar to them, that we'll also like." The more clients you have, the more likely this will happen. "In a firm of our size, we might get two referrals a month. But back when we had only 50 clients, we only got about eight referrals a year." So, if you're small, relying only on referrals can be a slow way to grow.

However, if you're very proactive on referrals, they can be an extremely powerful, efficient, and economic method of growing a beginning practice. For Amy Leavitt, early referrals were absolutely critical in establishing her practice. "I had a hard time breaking in to the market. But eventually I got a referral to someone and did a good job for them, and they referred me. Referrals were my sole marketing, and because I had no market, I marketed myself exclusively to existing clients. If they became raving fans and I kept them being raving fans, then I would be okay."

But for Leavitt, this was not an informal system, a vague hope for word of mouth. "I had a referral *process*. I let a client know when we became engaged that if we did an exceptional job, then I would ask for help with introductions. So I really made a good deal with them before we started: that if I earned the right to it, I would get their help."

In Hollywood, there's a saying that there's no such thing as bad PR. But that's just in Hollywood and just for actors. For planners, there is only positive PR, and referrals only work if you do a good job. People may talk about what a good job you do, but if you make someone unhappy, they'll also talk about you. What Leavitt said applies to almost any planner in any region: "If there is one person in Vermont bad-mouthing my company, I'm out of business."

Don't think that only clients can be sources of referrals. As mentioned in a previous chapter, Sheryl Garrett, when starting her middle-income practice, relied on referrals from practices that handled only high net-worth clients. Of course, to take full advantage of colleagues' referrals, you should be involved in professional groups. Garrett is involved in NAPFA, among other organizations.

In fact, Ed Slott says you can't overemphasize the power of colleague referrals. It's all about helping each other. "There's nothing better than helping other people. It comes back to you tenfold. The more you help others, the more you help yourself—so many people fail to grasp that." Too many are afraid to be first as well, standing there like a wallflower at an eighth grade dance, waiting to be asked.

"I used to do estate planning seminars," continued Slott, "and I said the key is to refer other people. Others said, 'Why should I refer to them, they never refer anyone to me?' Well, he's saying the same thing—so no one is referring anyone!" Slott said he's lost track of how many times he's referred a client to a lawyer or real estate agent. "If you do something like that for someone, they'll remember it forever, and it will come back to you."

# ADVERTISING
## Planners Go to Madison Avenue

The vast majority of this book deals with strategies for winning. However, this section on advertising is about a strategy that works only rarely and that has failed to catch on with most planners—probably with good reason. It's usually expensive, and the few who have tried it have not had much success.

Its reputation is almost tainted. Professionals have long eschewed advertising. CPAs, for example, were banned from advertising. Even when the ban was lifted, they weren't supposed to state in an ad that they were, "The best CPA in town!" because they weren't supposed to say they were better than a colleague.

There are practical considerations as well. "Advertising is a shotgun approach and does not come across as credible. Merrill Lynch can advertise because Merrill Lynch has a brand. Most planners do not," says John Bowen. Deena Katz concurs: "You look at TV and you can see all the big guys. In a one-hour show, you can see all of them, Merrill Lynch and the rest. But that's a repetitive market. You can see those commercials every time you turn on the TV. People get to know the name. That's really costly to have that kind of thing, and we don't have that kind of budget." If you're the right age, you remember the running bulls and the tagline, "Merrill Lynch is Bullish on America." Those ads cost millions to produce and broadcast.

You might be able to afford a newspaper ad, but if you put an ad in a paper once, no one will see it. "Financial planning is a crisis business," says Katz. "People have to reach some kind of necessary decision-making stage to decide to see a planner. The chances that they will have their crisis on the day you have your ad is real slim."

Advertising may simply be in opposition to a consultative financial planning relationship. Bill Bachrach says advertising is really the hallmark of a sales job. "If you behave like a salesperson—you resort to advertising, direct mail, cold calling, mass-market seminars, then you're a salesperson."

"I never ran an ad—I was just too cheap to advertise," says Amy Leavitt. Garrett, who is reaching out further than most other advisors because of her validator model, took a Yellow Pages ad, which she said pays for itself.

Morris Armstrong made a couple of forays into advertising but did not find it ultimately rewarding. "I list myself on a bar association Web site as a vendor, because I also do divorce planning. But I've gotten pretty much nothing from that. I did some tax prep work last year, and I advertised for that—also nothing. I do taxes mainly for my clients. I thought, because I had upgraded my tax software, I might as well advertise. I did five weeks in a local paper. It cost about $300, but it didn't even pay for itself."

Dan Moisand does limited, focused advertising. "First, if something happened that I wanted people to know about, that I believed made me unique in my area." For example, he took ads when he was listed among the top planners in *Worth* magazine and again when he was voted one of the Movers & Shakers in *Financial Planning* magazine. Wirehouses, he says, are already doing a lot of advertising that touts the benefits of financial planning. "And I don't have the budget they do. I'm not going to spend a lot of money duplicating the message that they're sending. And my time is better spent speaking with people directly."

I spoke to only two financial professionals who made major advertising commitments. Ed Slott shelled out $5,000 for a half-page ad in *Newsday*, a Long Island newspaper. Ric Edelman also markets himself through radio advertising and direct mail advertising. However, both of them advertised as part of a major, ongoing seminar program. If you're holding seminars, you need to promote them in some way (see the next section), but you are unlikely to need to promote them on the same scale as Slott and Edelman, especially while you're getting started. Save your money—there are better things to spend it on.

## SEMINARS
### Meeting and Greeting

These can be terrific tools for getting your name out there and meeting the right potential clients, but they are expensive and time-consuming events. If you don't do them right, you'll be wasting time and money. Seminars are distinct from speaking at an already planned event, sponsored by an association such as a bar association, FPA chapter, CPA society, or a consumer group. Virtually every planner thinks those sponsored engagements are a great idea, whether or not you get paid.

However, many remain lukewarm to the seminar concept, although some are enthusiastic and have used it to great effect.

Armstrong has done a few seminars, with "mixed results." For example, he specializes in divorce planning, so he's putting one together with a divorce lawyer. Sharon Kayfetz is not a big fan either and explains why. "Seminars are extremely risky. The bigger the area, with the more planners, the harder it is. Maybe they'll work better in a smaller city or town with less competition. You can buy mailing lists and join organizations and market them through the local Chamber of Commerce and Rotary Clubs. But seminars never worked for us."

Dan Moisand did them for a while but gave them up. "They're labor intensive, and I simply didn't enjoy them that much." He might have continued anyway—if they had worked a lot better. "But a lot of people were not there to find out whether they should become a client. A lot of times, it seemed they were there for food." Some people tried to come again and again for Dan's free meal. "There was no psychic benefit here. Yes, I'd occasionally get clients, but the energy was better spent somewhere else, and I haven't regretted not doing them in years."

However, Jeff Rattiner thinks they're a great idea. Because he has an education and training division in addition to his planning practice, he thinks a well-run seminar has a strong education role. "We're an information company, and that ties to education. Seminars and education go hand in hand. The nice thing about a seminar is that everything is pinpointed— potential clients can learn specifically what they need to know." And, presumably, sign with you afterward.

One of the strongest proponents of seminars in a traditional practice is Deena Katz. "Marketing is what brings food in the door, and one of the best ways to do that is to hold seminars."

Take the new tax act, she says. Which tax act? It doesn't matter. "There's *always* a new tax act. Learn about it and start talking about it." Today, she says, sophisticated mailing services arrange prospective attendees by demographics, including their assets and the kinds of homes they own—and their fees are within the means of small planning firms. "They can divide them by profession or Zip code—however you want to do it. They'll also do the mailing for you." All you have to do is design an invitation on your computer, have it copied at a Kinko's, and send the copies to the mailing service."

Lovas says that advertising your seminar can help in some markets, usually smaller ones. "If you put a flyer in *The Dallas Morning News,* nobody will see it. But this could work in a local newspaper."

The next step, says Katz, is to find a nice local hotel and tell them what you want. "There are lovely corporate people in every hotel who will find the right room for the right meeting." Keep it simple—there's no need for caviar and pheasant under glass. "If it's evening, serve a cheese platter and some fruit." If you want to be a big shot, you can serve wine, too. "For mornings, pastry and coffee are fine. But no big dinners—you'll gather a bunch of people who have nothing else to do and want to get fed. You want serious people only."

As a reporter, if I went to every food-oriented press event I was invited to, I could cut my family's grocery bill in half. One money-flush company apparently invited every business reporter in New York to the Four Seasons, one of the best restaurants in the city. Because it was the Four Seasons, everyone came, and, because they all came, they all wrote stories about the company? No. There was almost a tinge of desperation in the air: "You wanted us here *that badly?*" That's not the way you want to come across.

The key to getting people to show up is to get a hook, says Katz. "You need something people will want to know more about, because everybody holds a seminar. I'm in Miami, and you can go down Miami Beach, and every hour there's something going on and plenty of blue-haired ladies ready to line up for coffee and a Danish."

Look to affiliated companies for help. "Fidelity, for example, has a wonderful program called Practice Advantage," says Katz. "They have a whole seminar section in there, already written, with outlines and even sample invitations. It's really great. You want to run a seminar on retirement? Bing, there it is." You can get a lot of help these days, stresses Katz, so there's no need to reinvent the wheel. "And that's really important for people starting out. It's how much you can leverage your time—doing something that's quality and that's yours, but you didn't have to make up totally from scratch."

# SEMINARS FOR EXPERTS

When they work, seminars will attract people to contact you for appointments and become your clients. However, if you find yourself running really good seminars, they will not only *support* your business, they will *become* your business.

Ric Edelman began with seminars as a way to build a practice back in the 1980s. It wasn't easy, but it was effective. "The first seminars we created were for college planning. I used to teach them to PTA groups at elementary schools. I simply made phone calls to the local elementary schools, and they told me who the PTA presidents were. I called them up and said, 'I'm a financial advisor, and I'd be happy to provide a seminar at your next PTA meeting on how to save for college.'" They were ultimately receptive, although he had to explain patiently, again and again, that college planning really was for elementary school parents—by high school, it was too late.

"Most PTAs would only hold four to five meetings a year. I'd end up booking a seminar for six months out, and at the end of the PTA meeting, those interested in hanging around stayed for my seminar. We actually sat down and did a financial plan right there with them. I had all the worksheets and charts that I created, showing them, based on the age of their children, and whether they were going to go to a private or public school, how much they could expect college to cost and how much they needed to save on a monthly basis to get there. I showed them an overview of all the different investment opportunities—bonds stocks, mutual funds, and so on—and explained how each of them worked and how to evaluate what might be the appropriate way to go about investing." Parents expressed interest in making appointments, and that's how a $2 billion practice got started.

It sounds simple, but Edelman stresses that a lot of planning and effort went behind each seminar. "It was very cumbersome, for several reasons. It took months of advanced planning. A lot of effort was spent booking these events and developing the seminar. We had to spend a lot of time explaining what a mutual fund was—the fees, and risks, the expenses—a very laborious process. And the resulting client meetings would typically be two to three hours long because of all the education we were giving."

In the end, it was effective, he says, because he made it clear to his clients that he didn't care what they ended up choosing. He wasn't making a hard sell. The seminars, and his practice, were about education, not selling. "I said I was going to show them how everything works. And once you understand how it works, you can make an informed decision as to what's in your best interest and what works best for you."

The firm's reliance on seminars led to the creation of a nine-hour course on personal finance, taught three hours a night over three weeks. The seminars became so successful, they made the transition from free marketing tools to profit centers—he regularly conducts seminars for 500 people at $500 a couple. "We've done them on evenings and weekends and during the day. I do everything from a 20-minute luncheon talk to one event over a weekend for 6 hours each day. We've even toyed with the idea of overnight retreats—pretty much the only thing I haven't done yet."

However, even practitioners in small firms can deliver great seminars, as Ed Slott shows. He began his practice by planning and delivering top seminars and is now much in demand as a speaker. (Speaking for conferences is covered later this chapter.)

Slott, a CPA, began with a traditional tax practice on Long Island in a suburb of New York City. He wanted to be known as an expert in estate planning, however. "I had a tax practice but no specialty clients. No one knew I was a specialist. So I actually rented hotel rooms and bought newspaper ads about estate planning seminars. To get myself out there as an estate planning specialist, I *made* myself a specialist. This was the early 1980s, when no one was doing these seminars. And little by little . . . it happened. Consistency was key." And a willingness to spend. In the beginning, he admits he burned through a lot of money. Sometimes only five people showed up. "But I was doing it several times a month for years. Eventually, I became known. There was no magic bullet. Everyone asks me, what's the magic? It's just consistency and sticking to what you believe. Eventually, I became known as the estate planning guy on Long Island."

Actually, Slott is being modest. If you've ever seen one of his talks, you realized he approaches it more as a show than a lecture. IRAs are not the world's most exciting topic, but Slott realized he would have to make them interesting to attract people to his seminars, and he succeeded. I sat in at one of Slott's talks a couple of years ago. He didn't just read a prepared speech, he walked up and down the aisle, the accounting profession's answer to Oprah.

"When I was starting out, I used to go to technical seminars. I ended up saying to myself, 'This is boring. There has to be a place for a guy who can get this across and have fun with it. There's a real niche for a guy who can explain this and have fun with it.' That's basically what I do."

How did that approach lead to building a practice? In Slott's case, financial advisors started coming to his seminars, which led to other invitations at a local and then national level. When these purely educational and marketing events started encroaching on time he needed to spend on his practice, he discovered almost by accident he could *charge* for them.

You may not need or want to make a seminars a profit center in your practice, but you can certainly create one to garner more clients and gain attention in your town. Yes, they can be risky, but there are ways to increase the chances of success. Michael Lovas, a successful speaker himself, explains how.

First, he advises, think carefully about whom you want. "Many people have used invitation companies that promise to fill your room—and may do so—but not necessarily with people who will use your services or buy your products." Don't think that just because your room is full with any demographic group, that you have a success. "That's just idiocy," says Lovas. "If you connect with their emotions and do an impassioned job in your presentation, people will come up and want to book appointments, and you should have some way to service those people."

Build a psychological profile of the person you want to work with, he says, before targeting the Zip codes where they might live. "Recognize that you need to build this profile. If you don't do that, you just have a data dump. And that's not a very effective way to do business. Especially when you consider that your audience will quickly forget 75 percent of your data."

As the people start to arrive at the seminar, you should already be "on." Suggests Lovas, "Stand by the reception table or in the room and greet people when they come in. You have a limited amount of time. Everything you do, from the time people come in to the end, leads to the back of room where you set up appointments. Have an assistant take care of the administrative details while you talk to attendees before the talk even starts."

This is more than meet-and-greet time, says Lovas. This is time to *connect*. "Read the people as quickly as you can and say something relevant to each one." If you can read them, discover something about them, use it now. "Say something based on their type. It can double the number of appointments you'll get, if you can connect up front."

These connections also help once the seminar begins. You can give examples that are relevant. "Point to Bill, whom you just met, and say, 'Take Bill here. He's about to retire . . .' You are now connecting very deeply with Bill and anyone else in the room who happens to be in Bill's situation. But if you say, 'Let's say you're a wage earner, and you have one year to retirement and you're at 59½,' and start giving demographic data to show the category, it's so depersonalized it becomes meaningless. People don't resonate to this."

You have to connect personally and emotionally first, says Lovas. Only then will people pay attention to the facts and figures in your seminar.

# GETTING QUOTED

Did you see the movie *Being There?* The great comedic actor Peter Sellers plays a simple-minded gardener who is taken for an economic genius by the business and political elite. The President of the United States quotes him in a major speech on economic policy, then is horrified to find out that no one knows anything about him. "He has to be important," the President shouts. "I just quoted him on national television!"

That's the essence of getting quoted in a publication. Everyone is going to assume you're important, that you're an expert, if you are quoted in a publication. It will give you solid, instant credibility.

Although it's great to be quoted in a major national publication, like *The New York Times, Wall Street Journal,* or *Money,* getting your name in niche publications can give you the same benefit. In fact, sometimes the less-known publications can give you the biggest boost. It's the same thing with local newspapers. These may be little known outside of your town, but because you're operating locally, that's not a problem. It fact, it's a genuine advantage, because the local paper is the authority local residents accept. When Colonel Sanders of Kentucky Fried Chicken fame was still alive, local newspapers would send reporters to his home occasionally just to get his opinion on various issues affecting the town.

Larry Chambers is an expert on credibility marketing— gaining attention on the basis of your expertise, your credibility. At a seminar that I attended, Chambers brandished a technical publication for surgeons. "This is where you want to be published," he exhorted the audience. "Do you know what the average income of this magazine's readers is?" In terms of gaining credibility among desirable clients, that's the kind of magazine to be in. If you are quoted as an expert on financial planning for physicians, you'll be the one these high net-worth doctors call when they need advice.

With a little effort, you can become known to both local and national publications. Top planners have found these connections pay off. "The press has been among our best allies," says Sheryl Garrett. "We work with the local newspaper—they have a very proactive personal finance section. We do everything we can to maintain great exposure and participate in money makeovers." Nancy Langdon Jones has, as Chambers suggested, been quoted in a professional medical publication.

Lou Stanasolovich works closely with the *Pittsburgh Post Gazette*. In fact, he recently scheduled a breakfast meeting with one of the paper's reporters to discuss story ideas. Does this pay off? "Last year we had 231 interviews with the media." That's nearly one every business day.

"Get to know your local newspapers and their reporters," advises Katz. She and her husband and partner, Harold Evensky, have been quoted in dozens of major publications. "Become a resource for them. Let them know you're around, that you have ideas. We started out simply by writing to a local reporter, saying, 'That was a good article you wrote, and we liked what you said there, and the next time you want to revisit this, here are a couple of other things you might want to think about.'" Sharon Kayfetz did this, too: "I befriended a reporter. I called him right away when we set up our office."

Katz points out that, every day, some reporter is writing a finance story. Suddenly, the reporter says, "Oh my gosh, I need to have some attribution from somebody." Reporters keep lists of experts. (I have a list of over 200 experts to call on, organized by topic in my PDA.) Be proactive and read the paper every morning to find out what is going on. "Reporters call us all the time and want a comment on something."

It's also worth having a professional photograph of yourself taken. Publications often like to add a photo. Kinko's and similar companies can create a high-quality, digital version of the photo, which most publications can accept.

Every time something happens that affects our readers, I get calls and e-mails. A new tax law? CPAs with successful tax practices call me, offering to comment. The NASD proposes a new rule? Registered reps contact me to give their two cents. There's a contingent of federal groupies who e-mail me every time Allan Greenspan raises rates, or lowers rates, or leaves them alone. The point is, when someone gets in touch with me as I'm preparing an article, it's the easiest thing in the world for me to get a quote from them.

## THE PRESS RELEASE
### A Foot in the Door

There are a number of ways to get known to both national and local reporters—and I've seen just about all of them. I met pretty much everyone I quote in this book because they got in touch with me about helping with an article.

The most basic, traditional method of getting attention is the press release announcing expertise, plus follow-up. A press release isn't hard to write, but many people screw it up. It has to be short, simple, and clear. See Figure 4.1. (One part I left out that you may want to add is a broker-dealer affiliation. Broker-dealers may want to review any press materials you send, and some are quite anxious on this point, so check with compliance before actually sending anything.)

This sample press release does not overwhelm the reporter with technical details. The topic is clear, and contact information is easy to find. It's only one page long, so the reporter knows he can finish it quickly. It's easy to find out at the bottom who Jane Doe is and what her firm does. If this reporter is doing an article on 403(b) plans, or retirement generally, he will call her. If he's in a rush, he might not call her, however, but just use some quotes directly from the release—which is why Doe put them in there.

**FIGURE 4.1** *Sample Press Release*

For Immediate Release

Planner Addresses 403(b) Issues

August 9, 2003
Jane Doe Financial Planners
124 Maple Street
Anytown, Ohio 12345

*Contact:*
Jane Doe, CFP®
(330) 555-7246
<www.DoePlanner.com>

Jane Doe, CFP®, specializes in helping teachers with their retirement issues and has found a recent upsurge of concern. "Teachers wonder if they're going to have enough to live on," said Doe. "Even if they have secure jobs, often their spouses are out of work." Teachers have always assumed that a traditional pension plus regular 403(b) contributions would guarantee a secure retirement. "However, people are living longer and relying more on their own choices. Teachers, like everyone else, are confused about proper asset allocation. Is their retirement account growing fast enough?"

Doe sits down with her teacher clients and their spouses to discuss how to adjust contributions and make the right allocation choices. Doe finds that many young teachers are too conservative and many older ones take too many risks. "Teachers are getting even less advice than employees in the for-profit sector," she says. "And they are unfamiliar with the rules and opportunities surrounding 403(b) plans—the similarities and differences between them and the better-known 401(k) plans."

Doe has led several seminars for teachers in the Anytown, Ohio, school district and has made presentations on the 403(b) market for the Anytown chapter of the Financial Planning Association.

Joe Doe Financial Planners is a full-service planning firm serving teachers and other middle-income clients. Doe, a Certified Financial Planner™, has been a financial planner for 15 years and is a member of the FPA and the Anytown Chamber of Commerce.

You do need to think about how the publication you are contacting will want to make use of your expertise. To do that, you have to read the publication first. This sounds like a no-brainer, but many planners, even many expensive public relations firms, don't do this. Does a newspaper have a weekly financial planning column? You can suggest that reporter talk to you for a future article. But you have to know this. In a bad scenario, you can suggest that you be interviewed for the Sunday business section—only to be told the paper doesn't have a Sunday business section, something you should have known. The reporter is going to think you're an idiot, and he or she won't be far off the mark.

So you've done your homework, and you're now ready to send off your press release. Of course, the reporter is likely overwhelmed with press releases. I personally get about ten every day. Make sure yours doesn't get lost. Sending a press release addressed to "the business reporter" is a virtual guarantee that it will get thrown out. It looks like junk mail and will be treated accordingly.

If your first contact is the local paper—and that's a good place to start—find out who covers personal financial planning. If it's a very small paper, there may just be a general business reporter who covers anything business-related or finance-related in your town or county. Ask if this person should receive press releases for the financial planning column, Sunday business review, or whatever. Sometimes an assistant sorts and distributes them to the appropriate reporters. Ask how the contact likes to receive the press release—e-mail, fax, or mail. I prefer e-mail because it's easy to store and find later, but different reporters have different preferences.

Don't expect instant fame. "This doesn't happen overnight," says Katz. "You have to constantly work at it. You don't just sit down and write a press release on a weekend and figure your job is done. You have to follow up." Call to make sure the reporter got the release. You will likely have to reintroduce yourself. I get so many calls starting, "Hi, I'm Chuck. I sent you that release. Did you find it helpful?" Chuck? Instead, say, "This is Jane Doe. I sent you a press release last Monday about my work with 403(b) plans and teachers' retirement issues."

Also remain flexible. As in the sample, you may want to talk about your 403(b) expertise, but the reporter is doing an article explaining the different share classes. Because you are heavily involved in mutual funds, you can help with this. Of course, if it's a topic you don't know about, don't fake it. If you can, recommend a colleague with the necessary knowledge. You'll earn the gratitude of both your colleague and the reporter.

In the end, you'll likely get quoted, and this will snowball. The same paper will call you again because you were useful. Another reporter at another publication will read that article and, realizing you're an expert, call you as well. When I wrote for the *Journal of Accountancy*, I got a call from a reporter at *USA Today*. He was writing an article covering the same topic I had covered for a professional audience. After finding my article online, he was asking me for contact information for one of the experts I had quoted. So this CPA jumped from a professional publication to a national daily with no additional effort.

A couple of years ago, while writing an article about precious metal investing, I came across a gold trader who was quoted in several major publications. He told me that ever since he had been interviewed several years before, his popularity with the press had soared. He was receiving at least one press call a week.

One of the things I liked about him was that he called me back right away. Some reporters are on hourly deadlines—they call you at 9:00 AM and have to turn in the article to their editor by 3:00 PM. So, short of throwing a client out of the office, make getting back to a reporter a top priority, or the reporters will find someone else to quote.

"Getting quoted can give you credibility in an area where you don't have 'marble'" said Katz. "If you're Chase Manhattan or Northern Trust, you have marble." That is, a brand and a big edifice. Morris Armstrong is a sole practitioner with little time to do a major press push. Yet his work with divorce planning has garnered a lot of attention and was, in fact, recently quoted in *The Wall Street Journal.*

A more passive method, but one that can be extremely effective with a little work, is getting listed on your organization's press list. NAPFA, the FPA, and the CFP Board, for example, will help reporters find people to quote on a particular topic. NAPFA gives reporters a truly magnificent aid—a book, updated annually, with every member listed by state and area of expertise. The New York State Society of CPAs has moved heaven and earth to help me. They introduced me to Alan Kahn, a CPA with a planning practice who helped me with several stories—and ended up on our cover.

Another simple way to get noticed is a Web-based chat room. *Financial Planning* maintains rooms on various topics, and reporters troll these rooms looking for interesting threads that might make a news story. Often, they post queries: "Anybody here have any opinions on the Fed's recent rate drop?"

The sky can be the limit, if you're good at this. You can come to the attention of radio and TV stations. Ross Levin, Ric Edelman, and Alan Kahn are some of the planners in this book who have made it on the airwaves.

A few planners have hired public relations firms to do a lot of this work for them, but I'm lukewarm on this. A good firm is expensive. An inexperienced one will be learning about the financial planning market as it goes along—you'll be paying for their training. If you're small, and especially if you're starting out, you can do a lot yourself. Be your own PR rep first, and if you later want to move to another level, get a recommendation from a colleague. Lou Stanasolovich has had interns do a lot of the time-consuming PR work for him, and that might be a better idea.

Of course, there is no point in being famous if no one knows about it. Most planners have links, or at least lists, on their Web sites of all their mentions in the press. Put them in your brochures as well: "Richard Roe is a noted authority on tax-efficient investing and has been quoted in the *Anytown Bugle, Cardiac Surgery Today,* on CNN, and in *The New York Times.*"

## PUT PEN TO PAPER

The next step after getting quoted is writing articles yourself on topics on which you are an expert. This takes you even further toward getting established as an expert. There are a lot of venues for articles, from local papers to professional magazines. Ross Levin writes a column for the Minneapolis *Star Tribune* about one Sunday a month on a financial planning or investment management topic. Many magazines will sell you glossy reprints of your articles, which you can distribute to potential clients and at seminars.

Writing is really just an extension of getting quoted, and the same rules apply. Ask editors if they accept articles and what kinds of articles they are looking for. Some editors want to see an article, while others just want a proposal, so don't write anything until you know what they want.

Again, pay attention to the publication. If you see that your local paper invites local business leaders to comment on the economy every week, go for it. But a publication is not going to create a new section to accommodate your article. Also, make sure they haven't just covered your topic. Keep timing in mind: if you want to do a last-minute tax tips article to appear in March, that's great, but a monthly publication may have its March lineup finalized as early as January.

Ask your editor how long the article should be and what format it should be in, and pay attention. When an editor says, "That's a great idea. Can you write a 1,500 word article on it?" she means 1,500 words. Not 750 words. Not 3,000 words. Finally, you have to be on time. Publications usually run on very tight deadlines, and late articles are unlikely endear you to the staff.

Let's say your paper has a financial column with guest columnists. A proposal could read something like this:

> For the past 15 years, I have been a professional financial planner in Anytown, and I would like to run the following idea by you for your weekly column, "Money Views." My clients tell me that they don't understand what it means when the Fed cuts or raises rates. Should this change their investment outlook? Is this good or bad for business? I think an explanatory article about what the rate changes mean—and don't mean—to investors would be helpful. I will call you to follow up.

The planner expresses the idea briefly and clearly and establishes upfront that he is qualified to write it.

The same approach applies to a professional journal. An example of a really good proposal I got came from an expert on employee stock ownership plans. He told me—correctly—that it had been a long time since we had covered employee stock ownership plans. He explained why the topic would be useful to our readers. He showed me how his background and experience made him the obvious choice to write such an article.

A good query requires a lot of patience and perseverance. At *Financial Planning*, we may get a dozen or so proposals a week. Even if your article is terrific, there just may not be room for it right now, or the timing isn't right. Sometimes an article, if the topic isn't very time sensitive, will sit around for a couple of months. Then suddenly, an editor says, "Hey, we're short an article this month. We don't have anything on tax. Anybody send us a tax article recently?" And there you go.

It can be particularly hard to get an article into a publication if a well-regarded columnist already covers that topic. But, if one magazine isn't interested, another might be. If you have a facility for words and keep plugging, you have a good chance of getting your article published. Once the first article is done, you've established a track record that can make future placements easier.

These articles will eventually get you a lot of attention, but they won't make you rich. Publications generally make a strong distinction between freelance writers—who get paid because that's their job—and professionals, who do not. Yes, Samuel Johnson said, "No man but a blockhead ever wrote for any reason but money." But your "payment" is the publicity that comes from the article. Expect a small honorarium at most. A few planners, such as David Drucker, have transitioned to being paid writers, but they are the exception.

In addition to being nonremunerative, writing is difficult and time consuming. Many planners who enjoy making themselves available for interviews do not want to write articles themselves. Some people are better writers than others, and a primer on effective nonfiction writing is beyond the scope of this book. But, if it's something you think you're good at, it can be a great marketing tool.

## PUBLIC SPEAKING

For marketing purposes, I'm separating this section from seminars. The skills are pretty much the same, but by public speaking, I mean speaking to a conference where you were an invitee. That is, you have no organizational responsibility, and the main point is not immediately to get new clients but, as with writing and getting quoted, establishing your expertise—and associating yourself with the FPA, AICPA, or similar prestigious group.

Speaking engagements run from local business groups to national conferences. Many sponsors of the most prominent conference are nonprofit organizations, such as the FPA and

NAPFA, but others are run by deep-pocket financial corporations, such as Charles Schwab, so there is the possibility of substantial speaking fees.

But, as with writing and other PR events, you have to start small. Big, national speaking engagements come after you're known. My first speaking engagement was at a local chapter of the IAFP (which became the FPA). I was invited after one of the conference organizers read an article I had written. Subsequently, a state CPA society called me and asked me to do "something about the Web," because that's what I had written about.

Many, perhaps most, of the planners in this book have spoken at various conferences. Dan Moisand is always getting invited. "They come out of the woodwork. For example, one client is a member of a women's group. They need speakers. Once you have your talk, you can do it anywhere."

Few planners, however, have spoken as extensively as Ed Slott, who has gradually scaled back his accounting work to have more time to speak. His engagements not only earn him money but raise the profile of his practice. He has about 150 speaking engagements a year.

Slott admits he also became a speaker "almost by accident." In the beginning, like every speaker, he did it to market himself, but as he became known, he could increasingly charge for his speeches. "I didn't know what to charge. I threw a number out there. When they paid me, I thought, hey, that's a good number. Even now, you test the water. It's extremely lucrative. I think I first asked for $5,000, and I thought that was ridiculous. How do you go from free to $5,000? And then I started upping it . . . sometimes $10,000, sometimes more. And it's grown from there." He loves it. "We're actually booking a year ahead of time. I wish I could clone myself. It kills me when we turn down events because of scheduling conflicts."

There are speaker bureaus that can represent you, often for a commission of your speaking fees (see the Resources). Some of them specialize in the financial service professions. However,

Slott has never used them, finding their policy was something of a catch-22: they don't want to represent you until you have experience, but once you're known, you may not need them anymore.

Once you get an engagement, you need to take into account how you will present the material. First, rehearse your presentation. If it's a casual presentation at a local business association and you've been asked to speak for half an hour, 40 minutes is probably fine. But at a larger, scheduled conference, if you go over, you run into the next presentation, and that starts creating a speaker gridlock. Too short can be a problem if the conference organizers are offering your presentation for continuing education, because credits are calculated by the hour.

Speak with the conference organizer about question and answer time. A lot of questions after a conference is not a sign that you failed to address key points. Rather, it is a sign that you really reached the audience and they want to continue. If you can allow for Q&A, this is a great way to connect. In fact, after the formal Q&A period, smart speakers hang around the room for informal conversations with participants. The connection-building possibilities, after you have just wowed people with a good talk, can be excellent. This is true whether you are talking to potential clients, other business people, or fellow planners.

## A FEW WORDS ON NUTS AND BOLTS

Most likely, you'll be speaking from a podium in a hotel room with a microphone. Particularly if you're covering a technical topic, you may want to do a PowerPoint presentation. For this, you'll need the presentation itself, a computer, and a projector and screen. You can burn your presentation on a CD and use your own laptop, although the conference organizer may have a computer already set up. A projector that can connect to a computer tends to run to thousands of dollars, so this along with a screen are usually the responsibility of the conference organizer. However, you should confirm this beforehand if you need to run PowerPoint.

Before you actually create a PowerPoint presentation, you should know that some believe this is the greatest piece of software ever designed, while others believe it was introduced by Satan to wreak havoc on Earth. Some companies have banned it from internal presentations. It's true that some speakers rely on their slides too much, and too often speakers seem to believe that flashy displays will cover up a poorly organized talk.

However, I remember life before PowerPoint. The only way to get the graphical clarity was with actual slides. Producing them was expensive and time consuming. Only speakers from big corporations could afford them. PowerPoint has leveled the playing field. Anyone can have a well-illustrated presentation, if they can stop themselves from going nuts.

I worked in book publishing in the early days of desktop computers, like the Mac Plus. The Mac was a pioneer in offering a variety of typefaces, or fonts. Our authors thought that, if the Mac came with 15 fonts, they should find a way of incorporating all 15 into one manuscript. In multiple sizes. The result was a visual monstrosity. Today, most people know to set the typeface at Times Roman 12 point and leave it at that. In time, they will learn to do the same with PowerPoint—keep it simple.

John Olsen, a tech expert and a speaker, clarifies the plusses and minuses of PowerPoint. "You can sit in your home with PowerPoint and play with some great tools, like animation and 3D modeling. You can make presentations using the same tools as a Fortune 500 company." Actually, the individual can do even better. For example, Olsen recommends a dark background with light text, not the other way around. He prefers a dark blue background with yellow letters, especially in a dark room. Also, all capital titles are hard to read, especially if they're in italics.

Also, don't get clever with your audience. My wife teaches English in a middle school, and every year she has to do a unit on grammar, a topic universally despised by her students. She has put together some lively, funny PowerPoint presentations on grammar, with cartoons and sound effects. It never fails to be a big hit and gets everyone through what otherwise might be a dull couple of weeks.

However, you are not presenting to eighth graders, so don't pander. Olsen found this out the hard way when he was giving a presentation on annuities. With a specialized program, he created an animated figure who walked across the screen, turned to audience, and said, "Isn't it about time to give them a break," in a Cockney accent. "I thought it was as cute as hell," said Olsen. "Everyone raved about the presentation afterward. How did I make the little guy? And then it dawned on me, from that point on, they never heard anything I said about annuities. All they cared about was the cartoon. I dumped it and never used animation again."

## CUSTOMIZE YOURSELF

In the end, every planner has to craft a program to get noticed that conforms to their own practice and personality. But it's possible—and necessary. If any activity that doesn't involve sitting behind your desk frightens you—well, that's understandable. Comedian Jerry Seinfeld once observed that, according to a survey, more people were afraid of public speaking than were afraid of death. "That means, at a funeral, more people would rather be in the coffin than delivering the eulogy."

Fortunately, there's help and some resources in the Resources. As Deena Katz says, "You might want to take some courses in public speaking and media relations, because you're going to need those kinds of skills no matter what you do."

## THE GO-TO PLANNER

Remember Sophia from Chapter 1? She has begun her practice in a commuter village near New York. She already has several clients but wants more. She realizes she needs a bolder profile in the village and surrounding areas, but as a beginning planner, she doesn't have a huge budget. However, she makes a list of effective, low-cost methods to help her stand out.

Her first step is a phone call to the *Daily Tribune,* the newspaper serving the tricounty area. As with most small newspapers, national news comes from various news services like Reuters and Bloomberg, but there is a local business reporter, Jack Yardley. She has noticed his byline on articles on the bond issue before the county legislature and the ongoing debates over village property taxes.

"Mr. Yardley? My name is a Sophia Fitzgerald, and I'm a Certified Financial Planner in Baskerville working with a variety of individual and small business clients. I know you cover a lot of local business and finance issues, and I am available to comment on many of them. For example, I have clients wondering about when to refinance their mortgages or how tax changes in Washington may affect the economy here in the county."

"Well, thanks, Ms. Fitzgerald. I'm not working on anything relevant right now, but I'd like to have your name and number in case something comes up."

"I can give it to you now, and I'd appreciate it if you could share it with other reporters at the *Daily Tribune.* I'd also like to keep you posted on key finance issues—nothing overwhelming, but I may issue press notices a couple of times a month. Do you prefer them mailed, faxed, or e-mailed?"

"I'm completely an e-mail guy. Send them to JYardley@ tribunenews.com." She doesn't want to come on too strong in this first call or press for a commitment, so she thanks him and hangs up.

Now, of course, she has to start preparing material to send him. Sophia already has some clients with young children, who are spending a fortune on day care. They're confused about what is deductible for children at which ages and whether it's worthwhile to join employer-sponsored plans that pay for day care with pretax dollars. She writes up a one-page, double-spaced explanation of the issues surrounding the financing of day care and e-mails it to Yardley. Both her e-mail and the attached release include full contact information—office phone, cell phone, and e-mail.

But why limit herself to the local paper? Sophia visits the Web sites of all the major professional magazines—to which she subscribes—to see what's coming up in her areas of expertise. While she could just call and speak with an editor, Sophia saves some time by downloading each magazine's editorial calendar. This lists the principal articles, or themes, a magazine will have in the coming year. It's usually published in the fall of the previous year. She notices, for example, that one publication is having a special issue on small business planning in four months. Although this sounds like a long time in the future, there's a good chance they're already thinking about it.

She calls the editor in chief and introduces herself as a professional planner—and, of course, as a loyal subscriber. "I noticed you are having a special issue on small business coming up. I specialize in small businesses and have a number of insights. Also, I may be able to provide some real-life case studies. Can you connect me with the writer who is handling that story?"

"Thanks for your interest, Ms. Fitzgerald. We haven't started work on that article quite yet, and we will probably be giving it to a freelance writer to handle."

"Could you tell me when you'll be assigning it? I'd like to make sure the writer has my name."

"We'll probably be assigning it early next month. E-mail me your contact information, meanwhile." Sophia says she'll do that right away—but she knows the editor in chief probably gets a couple of dozen inquiries every day. So she makes a note on her calendar to follow up early next month to remind him.

Sophia is on a roll. She has a copy of *Florist Monthly: The Magazine of the Retail Flower Industry* on her desk, dropped off by her florist client. She calls that magazine's editor in chief next. "Ms. Rose? My name is Sophia Fitzgerald, and I'm a financial planner outside of New York City. I have a florist client who subscribes to your magazine, and I know you address the financial aspects of running a flower shop. I can provide some commentary for one of your writers or even write a piece myself. My client has made me aware of the special issues relating to running a florist shop, so I think I can provide some concrete advice."

"That could be interesting, but the last time we did a piece like that it came in so technical, it was incomprehensible by most of our readers. Could you write something at a real layperson level?"

"Sure. It's my job to explain these topics to a lay audience."

"Another thing is that our budget is very small . . ." Ms. Rose lets the sentence dangle, but Sophia picks it up.

"I understand. I'm more interested in getting my name out there as a leading planner for small business owners, so I'm less interested in payment than I am in getting a dozen or so free copies I can distribute."

"Well, let me consider that at our planning meeting in two weeks. Meanwhile, e-mail me a brief bio and contact info." Again, Sophia sends the contact info and makes a note on her calendar.

Now it's lunchtime. Sophia leaves her office and walks down the block to her friend, the lawyer. He was just about to go out to lunch himself. "Do you have a moment? I know you mentioned your bar association meetings often have a speaker on some topic of interest. I've been doing some estate planning work with some of my clients, and I'd be happy to address a future meeting."

"We have speakers every month, but there was a lot of unhappiness the last time we had a financial planner, about a year ago. It was supposed to be on some general issues but quickly turned into an infomercial for his services, and he spent the reception afterward pushing some damn annuity product on everyone. You're not going to do that, are you?"

"That's appalling. I can understand why everyone was upset. But for me, this isn't about getting new clients or selling products. It's about introducing you to some financial issues. Afterward, rather than handing out brochures, I'd rather hear from your colleagues about some of the legal issues surrounding estate planning. If your events chairman is anxious, I can send him an outline of my PowerPoint slides to reassure him." The lawyer gives Sophia the chairman's contact info, and then she goes out to lunch. Although she hasn't done a single minute of billable time this morning, she has been very productive.

Some weeks later, some of Sophia's efforts have borne fruit—although not in the way she expected. Yardley from the *Daily Tribune* called her suddenly, with just a hint of panic in his voice. "I'm hoping you can help me here. I'm on a tight deadline."

"So you're going to cover the local day care issue?" she asks.

"Oh no, not that, this is about something called a 529 plan. Have you ever heard of it? We just heard that Carollton-Garrity Food Services started offering an automatic deduction for these. They're the biggest employer in the county, and my editor heard about this and asked me to do a bit about these. Is this something you do?"

Sophia switches gears quickly. She has helped a few clients set these up. She doesn't have all the information right at her fingertips, but she doesn't want to lose this reporter now that she has his attention. "Yes, it's something I've been involved with. I can give you a brief explanation of what they are and how they work, including the tax implications." She gives him the same basic explanation she gives her clients—a five minute presentation. "I have some exact figures, such as the maximums in this state, and I can get you a complete list of the investment choices here, if you can wait an hour."

"Oh, just give me the Web site for the state plan, if you have that. What I would like is a comment on the choices Carollton-Garrity is offering. They're actually offering the Rhode Island plan only. Is that a better plan than New York? Is this overly restrictive of Carollton-Garrity, or is it generous that they're doing anything at all?"

As excited as Sophia is about getting quoted in a local paper, she doesn't let her enthusiasm override her caution. "Different plans could be better for different people. I've heard good things about the New York and Rhode Island plans, so I can't really say which is best in a given circumstance. It wouldn't be fair to comment on the company's plans without knowing the details. However, you can quote me as saying that, increasingly, companies are offering these plans, although I don't have any statistics."

Sophia gets two paragraphs in the next day's paper. She has a clip framed and hung in her office and starts a press clip file.

Later that week, she gives her presentation at the bar association, and it's a big hit. She mentions no products and scarcely mentions her firm or her services. But she engenders a lot of goodwill. Lawyers come up to her afterward to exchange cards and talk about the possibility of referrals. The visibly relieved chairman asks if she would consider doing a presentation with a local tax accountant about tax planning and tax-efficient investing.

On the other hand, she never heard back from either the professional planning magazine or the florist magazine. But PR is a matter of percentages, and she isn't doing too badly. She decided to give a reminder call to both editors next week, and already she has her first clip to show she is becoming established as a media resource.

At the end of the week, the president of the Baskerville PTA calls. "One of our members just saw that 529 article, and you were quoted. Would you have time to address our next meeting about how these work?"

## EXECUTIVE SUMMARY

- Marketing, sales, public relations—these are ways of selling yourself, which you have to do to become successful.
- Build a referral network—good clients come from other good clients and from colleagues. Some planners have a formal referral process.
- Advertising can work in special circumstances but in general shouldn't be necessary if you use other techniques.
- Seminars require a lot of work and can be tricky, but they can bring you a lot of attention and even transform your career.
- Build a good relationship with the press—getting quoted is an economical way to become famous and build credibility.
- Press connections require organization and persistence but are within the means and abilities of any planner.
- With a little care, you can create your own effective press releases, but remember that follow-up is key.
- If writing is in your blood, you can continue to build credibility by writing articles for professional or consumer publications. This is time consuming and frustrating, but the rewards can be great.
- Public speaking is another attention-grabbing technique and works both as a marketing strategy and as a profit center.

# 5

# MASTER OF THE HOUSE

**A** human resources consultant at a conference I attended swears that the following is a true story. He was giving a class on employee supervision to a group of high-level executives, and he asked, "What does it mean when I say communication between managers and employees is a two-way street?" One executive thought for a moment and said, "It means it isn't enough that I tell my employees what to do—*they have to listen.*"

Can you imagine what it was like working for that guy?

I can. I once worked in a department where the vice president was a tantrum thrower. If a report was late or she didn't get an expected callback, you could hear her screaming up and down the hall. After one particularly loud tirade at her assistant "to get me that damn paper right this minute!" I saw him sigh, get up from his desk, and walk into her office. In a quiet, even-tempered voice, he said, "Would it have killed you to say please?"

She at least had the grace to be embarrassed.

Don't be one of these managers. Although some planners practice alone, many have at least one assistant. As your practice grows, you may find yourself with a dozen or more employees. This experience can be difficult, because basic human resources management is not part of a financial planning curriculum. However, successful planners do manage their staff, either because they were naturals or they learned the hard way. With some practice, you can be as good a manager as you are a planner. Perhaps even more importantly, you can learn whether you want to have the kind of practice that requires you to spend a lot of time as a manager.

Look at it this way. "An independent financial advisor who hires a staff adds two dimensions to their own job," says compensation and human resources consultant François Quinson. "The first one is that he needs them to do the more mundane, repetitive, simpler elements of his own job. This would be true if the financial advisor were himself an employee in a larger firm, supervising others. The second dimension is that he is now an 'employer'—with the duties and responsibilities inherent in that role."

## THINKING ABOUT STAFF

As you prepare to assume that role, first ask yourself how big a staff you'll need. Staff size depends on how many clients you have, and how you plan to serve them. Mark Tibergien, of accounting firm Moss Adams, has spent a lot of time looking at practice management issues. Before you make a staff decision, think about your ideal number of clients and how much income you can expect. "You say that you don't want to grow bigger, but if I don't, you can't afford to practice. So you add an employee, and you have liftoff, but as soon as you add overhead, you have to sell more to cover that overhead. That becomes a big challenge for a lot of practitioners."

Start, says Tibergien, by defining which clients you want to serve and why and what that client service experience is going to be. "The client service experience will help you define your business model, what your staffing should be." Consider the optimal number of client relationships you can manage—actively manage, stresses Tibergien, not just have on the list. "It can be fairly revealing when you get down to it. How much time do you have in a day, what do you have to do for the client, what are their expectations? Is it possible to fulfill those personally, or will you have to add staff?"

As stated previously, the more complex your clients' needs, the more time you'll have to spend with them, but the more income you will get from each. "If you're in the affluent marketplace, then 60 to 90 clients is the optimal number," continued Tibergien. This helps you get a fix on your income stream and, thus, how much staffing you can afford. "It's like developing a personal financial plan for yourself. Do you know how to save, and what risks you should take? It all depends on what assumptions you are starting with. If you're not successful in business, what gives you credibility as a financial advisor?"

This may take a lot of thought and adjustment, particularly while you're getting started. Another consultant, John Bowen, advises erring on the side of small while you're going through growing pains. "Keep staff relatively small, very focused, creating a wow experience for your clients. Hire the necessary administrative support necessary to deliver that wow. Before you hire, consider outsourcing all but your core competency, which is often client relationship management. If you must hire, try to engage the individual as a consultant first. That way, you find out who could really work." Office temps and freelancers may cost more, but they're less expensive and less troublesome than a bad permanent hiring decision.

For example, you could hire a temp from an agency to get you through a busy period and to get a sense of what you can give to an assistant and what you would rather do yourself. Do you have quarterly invoices to send out? A freelancer may be able to handle this for you. In fact, this is an excellent way to move into permanent staff, as you and the temporary worker get to test each other for compatibility before making a long-term commitment.

Once you have a permanent staff, however, you have crossed a line. You are now a manager and have to act like one. "Show passion," says Bowen. "In a small business, lead by example. Share regularly and have formal weekly meetings. Remember, when employees make wrong decisions, it's often because they don't have the necessary information. So share the firm's financials."

## HOW BIG A PAYCHECK?

One of the keys to successful management, says Bowen, is the compensation package. You may be struggling to get your firm going, but Bowen warns, "Remember—your employees think you make too much." That's right, and you have to deal with that. Bowen suggests providing a bonus plan based on cash flow. "Say the financial planner earns $200,000. This money goes into the plan with other salaries. The profit left over comes out as bonus. This will help keep your employees focused on the bottom line with you. Don't just pay yourself what's left over."

The details of compensation, of course, are regional. (The FPA does a compensation study with Moss Adams, available for purchase through the FPA.) You'll have to pay someone more for a given job in New York City than you will in Baton Rouge. Although salary tables are available from both government and private sources, they probably won't be of much use. To see that a "receptionist" on average makes a certain salary in your city is too general. Will your receptionist have extra duties or just answer the phone and greet clients?

You can get some guidance from an employment agency. These often work on commission, so there can be a high, up-front fee compared with placing an advertisement in a local newspaper. But a competent agency will have a sense of how much you will have to pay for someone with a certain skill set and level of experience, and they will do the initial screening of resumes.

## GO WITH A PROFESSIONAL

For many planners, dealing with staff is going to be like dealing with technology—tough and something they weren't trained for—but necessary. "This is an issue for a lot of people. You need to decide where your highest and best use is," says Deena Katz, who has a staff of 17. "If it's not running a practice, you better hire somebody who can. If it's just you and an assistant, you should be able to handle it. Once you have to start adding different kinds of staff, you have HR concerns, compliance concerns, all kinds of things you need to deal with. If you're not a manager, hire somebody who is, like an office manager." When you get bigger, says Katz, you can get a chief operating officer—someone to manage day-to-day kinds of things."

Quinson concurs. "As your staff grows beyond a couple of people, you may want to have an office manager relieve you of most of the day-to-day administrative duties so that you can concentrate on your professional activities." But choosing this person is important. You need to select someone who brings solid experience to the job. "Whatever good or bad habits this person brings is what you can expect to be picked up by the rest of the staff, so make sure these habits are what you want. Even though you now have someone between you and the rest of the staff to manage their day-to-day activities, you are still accountable." He continues, "Delegation is not abdication." You still need to be intimately involved in managing the performance, not only of the office manager, but of the rest of the staff as well. Do it together with the office manager. Your employees' compensation, salaries, and benefits can represent a huge portion of your expenses, and you want to make sure you are getting as much bang for your buck as possible.

Katz also recommends looking into companies that let you outsource your HR tasks, such as payroll, hiring and firing, and health care. (See the Resources.) "It can be a great thing, getting that stuff off your desk," she says, because that's not what you may want to spend your time doing. Frankly, every minute not spent on what you are best at can be seen as wasted time.

Also, HR can eat up a lot of time—there are many requirements. Indeed, you assume a number of legal and regulatory obligations, points out Quinson. "They are potentially too perilous to be ignored, yet too complex to be mastered if the financial advisor is to concentrate first and foremost on professional activities." He also advises planners to get outside help from a consultant—or, as Katz suggests, outsource the whole human resources function. "Some firms specialize in providing this service to employers with just a few employees." (Some of these are listed in the Resources.) If you know something is not right but are not sure what you should do, says Quinson, get competent professional counseling. "Isn't that what you tell your clients? You are the expert when it comes to financial advice but may be an amateur when it comes to people management."

Whatever you decide, "The worst thing you can do is have a free-for-all," says Katz. "That is, allowing everyone to do their own thing and praying it works out. Because it doesn't. Everybody has their own agenda, and they'll follow it unless somebody tells them differently." Getting all that to work together is a big job.

"Most of the time," says Katz, "managing staff is like managing a kindergarten."

## EASY SOLUTIONS FOR SMALL FIRMS

Many planners have followed Bowen's and Tibergien's advice, as well as the guidance of other HR gurus. More than one have found a way to let others manage staff, like Katz suggests. But what's really interesting is how so many top planners found themselves winging it. They freely admitted they had few supervisory skills when they started. Some of them confess that they still have no skills. But they do have people skills or they wouldn't have been successful planners, never mind successful managers. They used these skills to learn the technical and psychological aspects of becoming supervisors.

"It's hard to do without anybody," says Sharon Kayfetz, "even if it's just one person." As noted in the technology chapter, she managed to reduce head count by going completely paperless. "We once had five people in the office, then down to three, now just one part-time employee and a scanner a few hours a week."

As a practical matter, she said, there's more to do when you're a boss. Like Quinson, she realized a supervisor has to handle a number of technical issues. "You have to be up on OSHA and harassment policies. Planners should check out the local Chamber of Commerce for technical help." That's where she was able to pick up a human resource manual and help with local regulations. "For example, you have to give each employee an unemployment booklet, and there are ergonomic advisories that have to be posted."

The Department of Labor Web site provides a thorough, well-organized reference for employers on a range of issues. (See the Resources for details.) It's useful even if you employ just one assistant or a receptionist.

However, the planners I spoke with, although not denying the importance of the regulatory aspects of HR, were more concerned with the psychological issues of management and the practical angles of supervising a staff. The smallest firms found themselves in the best position if they could find one person who could take care of the entire back office. Says Nancy Langdon Jones, "I had a friend who was retiring after a long stint at a large company—so I hired her to work for me. Ronnie became a paraplanner, and now she does everything for me. I can bounce ideas off her. She keeps me organized and makes me look good."

Ed Slott was equally fortunate with Laurin, his office manager. "She runs the whole office," he says, and she takes care of his extensive and complex travel arrangements. He also has an employee who handles his newsletter and accountants who work in his tax practice.

As you get a little larger, the issues become more complex. Decisions become harder, and you have to think about where you're going. "Supervision was one of the areas with which I have the least amount of comfort," admitted Dan Moisand. "In my first partnership, we had one full-time support for both of us, and that worked really well," he said. "After I went solo, I had a number of people that never did much more than part-time work. But I hesitated to hire full-time support. I hadn't hit the wall, but I could see it. I kept asking myself, should I bring someone in? I hesitated because of the supervision and training aspect."

He sees this as a key aspect of hiring: planners need to have an idea of what the training plan will be for the new employee. "What will you teach this person—and when? And how will you do that? That takes some effort. The cost involved in time spent can far outweigh the actual salary and benefits."

Moisand eventually merged his practice with another, larger firm. "Now, we have partners who enjoy that end of it." A great advantage, but Moisand advises, "Don't merge just to get support staff."

Sheryl Garrett has an unusual practice, and after coming to the conclusion that management was not her strong suit, she chose to solve her HR problems in an unusual way. "I felt comfortable with supervision—because I was completely ignorant. I'm a lousy manager, and I have resigned myself to it. Management of people and systems and things is not something I enjoy at all." So she cut the Gordian knot and hired people who didn't need to be managed. "I've surrounded myself over the years with self-directed professionals." Over time, she says, she's gotten better at choosing people who can work on their own. Eventually, as she grew, she was able to hire a de facto chief operating officer. "Last year, I brought in another CFP professional I'd worked with for years, and she basically is taking over my role in heading up the planning practice." This frees Garrett to do more strategic working with the network.

Jeff Rattiner doesn't much like supervising his employees, either—so he lets them do what they want. "I have six employees, and every one has a separate responsibility. I have someone responsible for financial plans, and someone responsible for tax returns, and someone responsible for investment management. And I try to coordinate all and act as a sounding board, but in essence I give them free rein to do what they need, when they need to do it. They have the complete authority to work within the boundaries set up within our system, for making things right for the client. This leaves me free to be the rainmaker. I try to bring in business on the advisor side and the consumer side, so we can keep things going and constantly grow."

But this only works, believes Rattiner, if the planner knows what the job should be. "I believe that if you need to do something properly, you have to do it yourself first. So I've done all the individual parts myself. Only after that could I delegate."

If you want to set up some good self-starters, like this, it also helps to have a job description for each employee, says Quinson. "Each job description should include a statement of the major purpose of the job. That is, in 25 words or less, state why the job exists." The planner also needs a description of the major activities of the job and three to six key end results or accountabilities of the job. "The key end results are what you use as references when reviewing the incumbent's performance. Their measures may be quantifiable—but if they cannot be quantifiable, they must still be objective and not subjective."

For example, there may be a lot of confusion and anger along the road if your secretary's job description simply reads,

"Generally maintain the office." However, if you agree at the start that the secretary should review office supplies every month and order those that are running low, refill the Pitney Bowes machine, and back up the client databases nightly, you have concrete items you can measure at review time.

A lot of this was new in the beginning to Amy Leavitt, who admits to an early ignorance on HR matters. She had to learn by doing. Although her practice is not as large as it was when she was actively growing it, at one point she had five full-time and two part-time employees. These included paraplanners who assembled the plans. Another employee was in charge of product administration—paperwork dealing with products, investments, insurance, all the underwriting, money transfers, and any administrative tasks surrounding updates on money managers. A client service specialist/general manager coordinated the workflow. "He was often on the phone first, so the client was greeted by someone who knew the situation. We didn't do that all the time, but we rotated this job." She had a secretary, a part-timer who did photocopying and filing. She had another part-timer for "special projects, things you never get around to, like setting up a referral database or something like that."

If you're having trouble figuring out what your employees want to be doing, or why you can't seem to keep a staff, see Figures 5.1 and 5.2.

It was definitely a growth process, Leavitt says, and the key was realizing that she was "a businessperson first, a financial planner second. I am a businessperson, a business owner, as well as a planner." The business couldn't run without a staff, so she spent time fostering a team environment. Losing a member of that team was as bad as losing a client—possibly worse. It was often easier to find a new client than a new employee, she found. "I treated my staff better than I treated my most valuable client. It was important to me that, if I'm going to invest in training, I couldn't afford turnover. I couldn't afford for them to leave."

**FIGURE 5.1**  *Why Do Employees Leave?*

The size of the last item may show that part of the problem is the principal's own fault. As Quinson says, "If an employee does not get it, it is usually because it was not made clear in the first place." That is, maybe the performance was poor because you failed to communicate. Interestingly, compensation is low on the list. You may be paying market salary and still have trouble holding onto staff. (Source: Moss Adams)

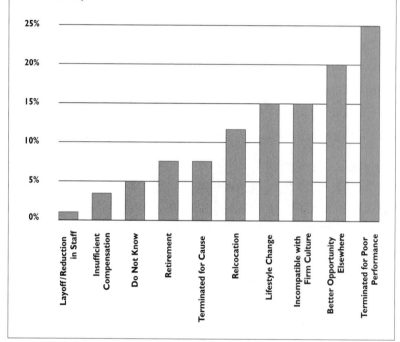

Because Leavitt was such a good planner, with the strong people skills good planners must have, managing people must have come naturally.

Well, no. "My personality is such that, when I get stressed, I get short. I want something *yesterday*, and I'm a poor communicator. I spent a lot of years feeling that I was being a jerk or apologizing to staff for being a jerk. So it was a growing and learning experience." Eventually, she learned to ask her staff to give her feedback, so she could help make their work environ-

**FIGURE 5.2**  *What Makes People Look for a Job Outside the Firm?*

Look at the bottom item. More than any other reason, your ability to manage is most important. Your staff has to have confidence in you. Promotions and pay have less of an impact than intangibles. Ross Levin noted that surveys always say that people are not money motivated; they're more meaning motivated. (Source: Moss Adams)

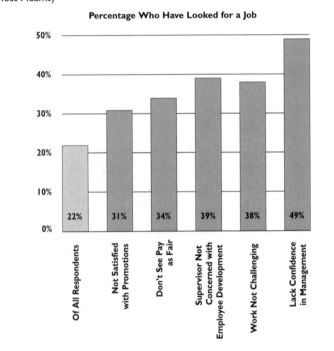

Percentage Who Have Looked for a Job

ment more productive and better. "I struggled with my own personality, because my employees are a vital part of my business. My profit margin would disappear if I had turnover, if I had to retrain people."

And, if she lost her employees, she knew she'd start losing clients. "My clients expect me to run a business." So she turned the tables and got advice *from* them. "I learned a lot—my clients are business owners. That was how I learned. I took the best among them. Who ran their businesses the best? When you walked into their office, how did they do things?" She simply mimicked her best clients.

Part of her plan to reduce problems in the office was cross-training, so that no gaps would appear if someone was out or overwhelmed. "This is the ooze theory of production—everybody oozed over to where the work was." In fact, this is an issue even with larger firms. "You know, part of the problem in most places is that one person knows how to do something, and when that one person is off, the whole place shuts down," says Lou Stanasolovich. "We're trying to teach everybody different tasks. We had classes on how to run the postage meter and how to send faxes out at a certain hour so the machine isn't tied up—on a delay mode. These things sounds elementary, but they sure improve your productivity." Stanasolovich faced these problems in his firm. The need to push for overlap is even greater when you're a small firm.

You have to communicate these needs, however. Quinson says that when you communicate with employees, they have a better idea of what they need to do. It sounds obvious, but in fact, many employers assume their employees are mind readers. "Handing an employee a job description is not enough. It has to be explained face-to-face. You have to be specific as to your expectations, explain in detail how you will measure performance against the position's key end results, and give feedback on a regular basis. An almost universal reason of why subordinates do not perform to their superiors' satisfaction is that superiors do not specify their expectations clearly, if at all. Make sure the employee has an opportunity to ask for clarification. If an employee does not get it, it is usually because it was not made clear in the first place."

Leavitt got the communication part right: today, Leavitt has summer reunions for current and even former employees and their families. "We have a good atmosphere, but we had to cultivate it. I think a lot of planners look at the business part as an annoyance. They devote as little time as possible to it, and that's a mistake."

Here's one final story from my personal experience. I worked at a small magazine, and one of our columnists was turning in articles so riddled with errors, I didn't know what to do. I went to the editor in chief to discuss it with her. She said she was busy that week. I said it could wait until next week, but we needed to talk. She said, "Richard, can't we just handle this by e-mail? I prefer just to handle these problems by e-mail." She so hated dealing with her staff, she couldn't stomach a face-to-face meeting. I didn't know what to say. In fact, I was still puzzling over this problem a month later, when the magazine—perhaps not surprisingly—shut down and laid off its entire staff.

When your employees want to talk with you, you talk.

## HOW TO GROW

If you choose to grow your firm to the point where it boasts a double-digit staff list, you will find yourself with some increasingly serious supervisory issues. You no longer have the same immediate contact with each employee as you would with just a few staff members. You've gone beyond having some basic support staff and are bringing on others to support you *professionally*. The planners running these larger staffs have to think about whom they're recruiting. Just as importantly, they have to think about whether these people fit into their firm culture and about how they can keep these employees happy and satisfied.

"Most planners can hire a receptionist and some basic staff," says Don Schreiber, who has 18 employees, "but that's easy." The hard part is replicating yourself, he says, because you only have so many hours in a day. "The planner is the main cog. Everything comes through the planner. Some may like this— but I think it's like being in Death Valley without a canteen. Every new client bleeds you. They become creditors of your life. The more successful you are at attracting new clients, the worse it gets."

The solution, as your firm grows, is to clone yourself by hiring someone whom you can train and mentor. "I look at recent grads from financial planning programs—the next generation of CFP's. They're well grounded in basic financial planning knowledge, but need to learn how to build a plan and work with clients." Think of hiring these new planners as hiring your eventual replacement. Says Schreiber, "The time you spend on training and mentoring may ultimately take away from current sales, but in the end, you increase your practice." Gradually, you introduce clients to a second tier of responsibility—you delegate. As the new hires transition, working with clients, they become steeped in knowledge.

But handle this delicately. Don't let a client think they've been "demoted," because they no longer speak directly with you but with a new associate, for example. Assure your clients that you are still the one behind the scenes, that you are still looking out for them. You can explain the change in positive terms: the new associate can take care of the client's immediate needs, while you spend more time on portfolio design. No one wants to hear that you're stepping back from client contact to spend more time marketing or to deal just with the "important" clients.

No matter why you bring on a larger staff—business development, speaking engagements, or investigating new hedge funds—the reason had better be clear to you and your staff.

Like Quinson, Schreiber believes a job description is essential. "You need one for everyone—including yourself." How can you possibly know what to delegate if you haven't decided what you want to do? A job description for yourself helps you define what your core function in the firm is and lets you delegate noncore functions. "Give away a slice of your own job description. You will become more effective." Schreiber looked at large companies and spoke with clients to gain HR insight." His firm doesn't have a dedicated human resources manager, which

Schreiber believes only becomes necessary when you have about 50 employees.

Ross Levin has a firm with about the same number of employees as Schreiber, and like Schreiber, he doesn't have a full-time HR manager. Someone in the firm manages that end of the business, however—and it isn't him.

I asked every planner I interviewed for this book how they grew into the role of manager. "I *never* grew into the role of being a manager!" says Levin, with a laugh. "I'm still bad at it. Because we're not big enough to have a full-time manager, we have different people doing different management responsibilities. Will Heupel, my business partner, started off doing a lot of management because he was better at it than I am."

Later, they brought in a third principal, Kathy Longo. "She does a lot of the management, and she's also better at it than I am. Ultimately, we'd love to have another layer, another person in there." He referred to Jim Collins <www.jimcollins.com>, the guru of successful companies. "At an FPA presentation, he said that you have to find the right people first. Get them on the bus and get them on the right seats on the bus." Levin also quoted Mark Tibergien. "He said to me once, you can never motivate employees, you can only *de*motivate them. His point was that you have to hire the right people who are intrinsically motivated. If you have the right people, then management becomes less of a burden."

Also reducing this burden is ongoing documentation and— Quinson continues to emphasize—communication. "This way you can objectively reward performance," says Quinson, because you're keeping track of achievements and know what your employees are doing. "Rewards include salary increases and bonuses, of course. But this is not enough. It is very important to say thank you as often as you can and to seek your employees' opinions on how things could be done better in the office."

On the flip side, continues Quinson, if you have an employee who isn't performing, the documentation helps you figure out what corrective action to take—and, if worse comes to worse, justify a dismissal. "Do not let things fester. People need to be managed. If you think there is a problem, address it. It won't go away unless you do. It will only get worse. Be proactive, not reactive."

Even though Levin has grown well beyond the one or two assistants stage, where he worked closely with a very small staff, he still makes sure he communicates and connects with his employees. In fact, he finds communication to be more important than ever. "A couple of times a year, we do a philanthropic event where we close the office during the week and work at an organization similar to Habitat for Humanity. The whole staff does this. Surveys always say that people are not money motivated, they're more meaning motivated. That's really been a nice thing for our office. It makes people appreciate what we have and gets us all together in a setting where we're clearly all equals. We're *all* hauling garbage and whatever, and we're doing it all together."

A couple of times a year, his firm also has a company social function, planned by the staff. "The staff picks the charities we work with and the charities. They also plan the social outing. We did a scavenger hunt at the Mall of America once. Last year, it was a St. Paul Saints game." Even if it's just a long lunch at an upscale restaurant at the end of the year, your employees will appreciate it. Such a token of appreciation can create a level of loyalty that is out of proportion to the cost of the meal.

## CONSIDERING INTERNS AND AN "OPEN OFFICE"

Stanasolovich says he grew into the manager role—but few planners have grown into it more completely or have taken it more seriously, with more profound results.

"I've been reading things like *Inc.* magazine for 20 years. I'm an avid reader, and I see things that people have already experienced." Like Leavitt, he has a lot of clients with their own businesses. "You have to ask yourself, do you want to be dedicated to being a good manager? Do you read about HR issues in magazines and newsletters?" You have to be aware of what's going on, he says, "and the better manager you wish to become, the more informed you have to be."

As an "informed manager," he's made some unusual moves, but they've worked well. "We run our firm by open book management. That is, the whole staff discusses everything openly, including salaries. We're all aware of each other's salaries—and the staff even votes on mine!"

Stanasolovich schedules monthly staff retreats to discuss various issues. "Everybody knows the financial statements. We run budgets quarterly, and we review monthly financial statements. We're always talking about what we can and can't do, any kind of major expenditures we discuss. Frankly, it keeps me from going off on odd ideas. A lot of business owners, left to their own devices without a group to discuss things with, sometimes don't see the business from all aspects." But, because of his close work with his staff, he says, "I think that's what I'm fairly good at—looking at all angles."

Another HR area where Stanasolovich really stands out is in his use of college interns. Not only can they handle a number of tasks in a cost-effective manner, but they serve as a pool for future permanent hires. Over the past nine years, he's hired about 40 interns, 9 of whom became full-time employees after graduation.

Almost any firm can do this. Official CFP courses are taught at colleges all over the country, but even if there isn't one nearby, you can still run an internship program. In fact, there isn't a CFP program near Stanasolovich, but that hasn't stopped him. "Most of our students come from Duquesne, in Pittsburgh. We presently have four finance and three marketing interns." In the beginning, they just called the university. Now, it has recruiting fairs several times a year that they can attend, and some schools have electronic internship posting boards.

Usually, Legend hires sophomores or juniors. "But never seniors—there isn't enough time to train them." In the summer, they work 40 hours a week, and during the school year, they average 15 hours a week over a term. Basically, the internship is about 1,000 hours a year.

"It's like getting 3.5 employees, at a relatively low rate. They build their skill set tremendously. We hired two new finance interns a month ago—high quality people, 3.6 to 4.0 grade point averages for the most part. They're assisting with running reports and doing billings, client preparation for meetings, and clerical tasks, too. In addition, they're learning financial planning, how to put together balance sheets and those kinds of things."

But, if you want useful, satisfied interns who may develop into employees, you have to invest in training, Stanasolovich stresses. "In fact, in their first month, about half their time is spent in training classes." He keeps a close eye on the work mix. "For example, I saw an employee stuffing envelopes the other day, and I said, 'Hey, get an intern for that. You oversee it—but get them to do that.' It's about leveraging time. Why should I be making copies? But still, we do try to limit an intern's time to no more than 20 percent on clerical."

Stanasolovich hires two kinds of interns: marketing and finance. "The marketing interns are writing and proofreading letters and pitching stories to reporters. One intern is in charge of electronic newsletters that go out to 15,000 people. Because we're part of the NAPFA media network, she takes care of the media requests." Another intern is great at grammar, so Stanasolovich has her checking every form letter. "They all do some aspects . . . some do print ads or the monthly client letter. And all set up press interviews and write pitches."

I can personally attest to the success of the marketing interns. When I first spoke to Stanasolovich for a story, I thought his firm was much larger than it was. I was speaking to a coolly competent staff member who was coordinating all press contact for Stanasolovich with the same efficiency I was used to when arranging to speak with a fund manager at a large investment company. I figured that only a very large organization could have such a an efficient marketing and PR department. But it was simply the effective use and training of interns.

As for the finance interns, "First, they get a lot of filing duty—matching confirmations to make sure trades went through correctly, crosschecking to assigned cost basis, and so on. They build a lot of cost basis information for clients—because when they come in to us for the first time, they usually find a mess. The interns can straighten it all out." Stanasolovich has them prepare investment management reports and client presentations, as well as doing a lot of daily research tasks. "The extra help cuts down on mistakes." As finance interns become more experienced, they move into financial planning area and work on basics like balance sheets and support pages. Later, they get involved with tax projections.

"Interns also work on parts of our budget. It's amazing what you can give them. The finance interns are writing summaries of our calls with portfolio managers at mutual funds. We have calls with portfolio managers, which benefits everyone. We have them do that. If there's a new manager we want to look at, they're responsible for contacting the manager and having a questionnaire filled out, following up, and setting up a conference call so we can do our due diligence."

The internship program has left Stanasolovich with more time for high-end marketing and strategic planning. "It's been a very fruitful process for us."

## RUNNING A MIDSIZED COMPANY

As firms get even larger, levels of efficiency can increase, even as the layers of complexity multiply. Look at Ric Edelman, who has about 90 employees and 8 temps. "We have 18 financial advisors on staff. I have two loan officers in my mortgage company and two insurance experts. The rest of the staff support those professionals and their activities. We have, for example, four people who work full-time at the front desk. All they do is answer phones and greet clients." There are six employees in his communications department and seven on his information technology staff, including four full-time programmers. It's a lot of people to keep track of, but keep in mind that with that level of support, the planners don't have to do anything except planning work.

It's part of Edelman's overall philosophy. "I have focused on the need to spend as much time and energy on entrepreneurship and business management as on financial planning. So we devote a substantial amount of energy to operating the practice and focusing on practice management issues, which many planners, I have found, ignore."

He thinks it's ironic that planners counsel their clients on hiring on advisor, yet they don't take that same advice. "You need to hire an office manager. Hire a marketing staff. Hire an HR manager and an IT manager, instead of trying to do it yourself." It's a refrain a lot of planners have sung before—sticking to core competencies—but few have taken it as far as Edelman.

"Why are planners out there buying and installing their own computers and phone systems? Why are they trying to design their own advertising? They don't know anything about those fields. The main reason we find that they're unwilling to hire outsiders or staffers is that they don't want to spend the money. They have an incredible aversion to investing in their practice. And the one thing I learned very early on is that I can't spend enough money. The more money I spend, the more money I earn." He asserts, "Many people look at the fact that I have 90 employees, and they cringe. Why would they want to do that? You have to remember that, every time you hire an employee, you make *more* money. The real question is not, why would you want any? The real question is, *how many can I have?*"

Delegating tasks is not new, either, and Edelman doesn't claim it is. "This has been in business management textbooks going back 30 years." But he has taken it to an extreme. "There's an incredible amount of work that has to be done, but not by you. In our practice, we have one simple rule: our financial advisors must devote 100 percent of their time either to talking to their clients or preparing to talk to their clients. That's all my advisors do. They're in constant communication with their clients, either on the phone or in review meetings, or preparing to get on the phone or have a review meeting. Everything else is delegated to support staff. We have a large amount of support staff as a result."

A given planner in Edelman's firm will have an assistant planner, an associate planner, and an administrative assistant. That's in addition to the operations staff. "All the paperwork and service needs are taken care of, so planners can be focused entirely on the advisory function. They're not dealing with the service or administrative function. Why should planners be typing their own letters and mailing them themselves, when they could hire someone at $20 an hour to do that instead?"

That leads to some interesting conclusions on planner/ client ratios. How many clients can one planner handle? Tibergien has made some good estimates, but the ratio ultimately depends on what else a planner has to do. "Some people might look at my staff and say, 'Each of your planners has too many clients—how can they provide service?' We find that we're providing far higher degrees of service, far more frequent levels of contact, than most planners, because my planners aren't doing anything that isn't client related." In a smaller firm, they may be so busy paying the bills, dealing with vendors, answering phones, or doing paperwork that they don't have a lot of time to talk to clients. "We have structured our environment here so that all of that is taken away from the planners, so they can deal exclusively with clients."

This approach leads to a strong sense of uniformity, of which Edelman is proud. In fact, uniformity is neither a good nor bad result. It relates to your practice philosophy. When a client calls Edelman for the first time, the call will be transferred to a planner. A brief conversation leads to an in-person appointment, and one or two others, as needed. When the client is ready and willing for implementation, the planner goes ahead, backed by the support staff. "Everything we do is uniform—from philosophy and methodology to implementation."

It's a far cry from the one or two assistant model of the small planner. Interestingly, the results can be very similar. Edelman's planner/client ratio can be seen as comparable to the ratio in smaller firms, when one considers that Edelman's planners have no responsibility other than planning tasks. In a small firm, the planner may have fewer clients but also has to spend time as the marketing director, PR director, and—of course—HR manager.

The question again is: what do you want to do with your life and with your practice? If you like being a planner and you don't want to spend much of your time managing other people, you may decide to keep your practice small. Or you may want to hire someone in-house to take care of those details. It could be expensive to hire someone at that level, but if they let you lead the life you want with the practice you want, that may be a good decision.

I spoke with a young CPA who had recently joined his father's well-established firm. The two of them realized quickly that, although both were very competent accountants, the father's skill was in the minutiae of tax code. He enjoyed them. The son loved getting in front of clients, discussing their fears and problems, and bouncing tax strategies back and forth. This partnership, these job descriptions, worked will for them.

As Ed Slott grew his practice, he spent more and more time writing and speaking and less and less time in his practice. A drawback? A mistake? Not for Slott. He enjoys his speaking and writing and finds it works well, funneling the clients to his staff. In fact, this is the first year he didn't personally handle a single return. He took a look at what he wanted to do and kept going. That's what every planner has to do.

Yes, you become a manager with even one employee. But how much time you want to spend on managerial tasks rather than on planning tasks is a function of your practice. It's your decision. The only mistake is moving yourself in a direction in which you are not doing the tasks you want to do.

C *a s e* S *t u d y*

## LEARNING TO BE A BOSS

Bob Wells has been practicing for several years in a two-room office in a major city. He's been happy on his own, but lately he's been feeling pressured. His practice has been thriving, but he realizes that he's spending more time on clerical tasks, so even though his income is up, his hours have extended well into the evenings and even weekends to keep up. Bob knows he can't keep going like this—he'll exhaust himself and won't be doing his clients any favors, either.

Some of his colleagues have solved the problem by reducing the number of clients they handle, but Bob doesn't like that idea. He'd still have to take care of the clerical tasks with the clients he has left, and that's what he's trying to avoid.

There's no two ways about it. He's going to have to hire an assistant. He doesn't have to move, however. The anteroom has already been an informal waiting area and storage room for his filing cabinets. It wouldn't be much work to fix it up for an employee. It's worth exploring, anyway.

He makes a list of things he'd like a secretary to do: greet clients, keep track of his schedule, take care of invoices, and order supplies. When he writes up a financial plan, he'd like his assistant to format it neatly. He'd like to be able to scrawl changes on his PowerPoint presentations and have someone else neatly enter them. It would be great to have someone intelligently screening his calls as well. ("Always put through a client, unless

I'm with another client. And here's a list of fund wholesalers I *never* want to speak with.")

He also has special projects. He keeps meaning to take charge of his PR efforts and compile a list of reporters who might want to quote him. An assistant could take care of that, too.

Bob is emboldened to write a want ad to run in *The New York Times.* (If Bob were old enough to remember a less enlightened time, he would ask for what used to be called a Guy/Gal Friday.) "Busy financial planning firm wants assistant/receptionist. Must be willing to work with little supervision. Must have fast typing skills. Knowledge of Word, Excel, and PowerPoint essential. Salary—"

Well, what about salary? Bob has no idea what he should pay. He could ask for salary requirements, but he might end up with such a wide range, he wouldn't be able to make a decision. Also, what kind of person is he going to get? If he's honest with himself, he envisions a superresponsible woman who quit a sec-retarial job 25 years ago to stay home and raise children, who is now looking for a job to augment future retirement plans for her and her husband. Bob also knows that if he vocalized this preference, he'd probably be violating more discrimination laws than he could count.

Maybe he needs professional help.

He takes out the Yellow Pages and calls a couple of agencies, asking how much they would charge to find him a secretary/ receptionist. The answer turns out to be a substantial portion of their annual salary, but Bob thinks the expense will be worth it. One big agency sounds like they can really help him and in-vites him in to discuss the details of the process. They go over all kinds of questions—what salary Bob expects to pay and what he can expect from a given range? How much vacation is he of-fering? Can he provide a health plan? A retirement plan? Bob knows what he's set up for himself and has thought about how he can extend these benefits to any employee.

"You know," says the counselor at the employment agency, "you can't offer the same kind of benefits that a big company can offer. But maybe you can offer other things. I can get you a recent college graduate who meets your qualifications, if they can get a chance to learn the business. How about you offer to pay for some courses leading to a CFP designation, which is what you have. Say you will start doing this after the first anniversary of employment. That gives them an incentive to stay. If you agree, I'll list this job on our books as 'college degree required.'"

"Send some people for me to interview," says Bob, cautiously, "and we'll see how it goes."

Over the next few weeks, a parade of young graduates files through Bob's door, all of them wearing severely tailored, brand-new suits. A lot of them are less than enthusiastic, clearly hoping for something a little more "Wall Street" with lots of designer furniture, a cappuccino maker, and a Bloomberg terminal in the corner. Bob has none of these amenities.

But one young economics major, Mary, seems intrigued. "So, if I'm the only employee, I'll have a chance to learn all aspects of your business?"

"You'll be typing and reading financial plans to start, and eventually I will ask you to sort all the correspondence and phone calls I get, based on what is useful for this practice. I want to emphasize that, particularly in the beginning, there will be a lot of clerical work. But if you're still interested after a year, I will pay for training toward your CFP certification and various securities or insurance licenses."

After she leaves, Bob tells the agency he thinks Mary should do well. They agency makes her an offer directly, with Bob's authorization, and she says she'll start in two weeks.

Until now, Bob has only thought in terms of generalities, but now he has to be specific. Mary will need to know exactly what she needs to do, starting the first day on the job. And he's going to be a boss, which means periodic performance reviews. He takes out his original list of duties and starts making sublists.

For example, he'd like Mary to keep track of all office supplies. He makes a list of all the key items so she can audit them every week and order whatever is running low—printer paper, water for the cooler, legal pads, etc. He also wants her to back up key files onto CDs every week. Bob has a safe deposit box across the street where he stores the back-up CDs. He'll put Mary's name on the card, and she can take care of this task on Friday afternoons.

The list ends up including every little task that Bob hates doing. To avoid overwhelming Mary, he selects the most important. As she becomes used to the position, and he becomes more used to her abilities, they can come to an agreement on how her duties will expand over time.

On the first day, Mary shows up early and eager for work. They take care of the W-4 form and other regulatory issues. (That was another benefit of going through a good agency—they went over the regulatory HR basics for him, so he could have the necessary notices set up before she started.)

They go over the list step by step. Bob has had to make some changes in the financial plan of a client, he gives Mary the marked up document to type in a proper format. He tells her a new client is coming for an initial interview at 10:30 AM. "One of the strictest rules is that I am never to be interrupted when I'm with a current or prospective client. It has to be a matter of life or death. Understood?"

"Absolutely," says Mary, who notes the rule on a pad on her desk.

The 10:30 AM appointment arrives—a husband and wife. Bob has told Mary she is to call him when an appointment arrives—he will personally meet everyone and bring them into his office himself, and Mary will get the coffee. At first, Bob feels a little awkward having someone else in the office. But Mary efficiently takes everyone's drink order, delivers them, and quietly closes the door behind her.

Ten minutes later, the interoffice ring on his desk phone buzzes. Bob ignores it while he talks with his prospects. Two minutes later, Mary meekly opens the office door. "I'm so sorry, but a Mrs. Michaels called, and—"

"Just take a message, Mary, and I'll get back to her as soon as I'm done." Bob feels tense, and he knows Mary feels the tension.

The rest of the meeting goes well. The prospects seem pleased. Bob asks Mary, who has taken over his contact management system, to help them set up another appointment in the near future, and she almost stumbles over herself in her eagerness to make up for her past transgression.

After the couple leaves, Mary speaks before he even has a chance to open his mouth. "I am *so sorry* Bob. But she literally said it was a matter of life and death and . . ."

"Mary, Mrs. Michaels has been a client of mine for 15 years and has a 'life and death' situation virtually every week. Alan Greenspan changes the rates, or doesn't change the rates, or whatever, and Mrs. Michaels has a heart attack." He takes a deep breath. "But there is no way you could have known that."

"It won't happen again." Bob knows from her tone that it won't.

The rest of the day goes without incident. At 4:30 PM, Bob tells Mary that the next morning, as a top priority, she should cut and paste addresses from the contact manager into a form letter he's going to give her. This goes out every quarter with the statements to all of Bob's clients.

"I don't understand," says Mary, looking perplexed.

"It's really simple. You copy the name and address and paste it into a form letter. You do know Microsoft Word, don't you?"

"Well, yes, but why don't you just do a mail merge? It takes half the time. You just put a little code in the form letter, and it can integrate your addresses from Microsoft Outlook into the letter . . ." Her voice drifts off. It's Bob's turn to look confused.

"Well, if you know how to do that," he says lamely and goes back into his office.

On Friday, the mail-merged quarterly reports have gone out—a day earlier than usual. Bob is leaving the office on time, now that he has help. Mary is more confident and no longer asks him if he prefers silver or copper paperclips, and she's become surprisingly deft at handling Mrs. Michaels. On Monday, he's going to start her on the PR project.

The employment agency calls Bob to ask how it's going. "She seemed very bright to us. Has she learned a lot in the first week?" asks the counselor. "We both have," says Bob.

---

## EXECUTIVE SUMMARY

- Once you become a supervisor, you have practical and legal responsibilities.
- Staff size is a function of what kind of practice you have and how you want to practice.
- Start small, and use temps and freelancers to get started. As you start to hire, write clear, detailed job descriptions.
- Settling on a compensation package can be difficult; a local employment agency can help you figure out how much you need to pay.
- Once you have even one employee, you have to train, motivate, and supervise them. Ongoing communication and documentation is essential.
- You have to be a leader, and if that's a difficult role, you can get a partner or COO-type employee who can handle it for you.
- Outsourcing HR functions can save you a lot of time and trouble.
- A good source of HR advice can be your small business clients.

- As your firm grows, you have to think about how to recruit employees who fit into a firm culture.
- One solution is to hire recent graduates and college interns, who eventually may become permanent employees. Training takes time but can be worthwhile.
- If you are an excellent manager, you may find that each employee adds to your bottom line by freeing professionals for key planning tasks.

# 6

# SCHMOOZE OR LOSE

I'm just a simple journalist, and I've never had to sell an investment product or service. It's hard enough selling my articles. But I had an amazing epiphany when I had my first summer job at 15, working at a lakeside marina in upstate New York. All I did was remember a customer who had rented a boat in July when he came back to rent a boat again in August. "Good to see you again, Mr. Jones," I said. He was thrilled at being remembered, and I pocketed an extra-large tip.

Of course, if someone has entrusted half a million dollars to you, you're going to have to do a little more than remember his or her name, but the principle is the same. Your clients want to know they are on your mind, that they are important to you. It isn't enough that they *are* important, however. You have to show them they are important. This is more than just good business sense; it's about creating a line of communication with clients that remains open, even when you don't have a key piece of information to impart to them.

These "reaching out" moments can be as simple as an e-mail or a printed newsletter, or even an envelope with newspaper and magazine clippings that might be of interest. They can be a phone call or a face-to-face meeting. But you need to think about what is best for your practice and about what your clients would like. From occasional phone calls and e-mails to elaborate thank-you dinners, there is no one right way to reach out. I worked some years ago at a family-owned company. One member of the family was a huge opera buff and had some of the best seats at the Metropolitan Opera House; another was a baseball fanatic and had box seats at Shea Stadium. The company's best customers thus had a choice of where they wanted to be thanked.

Just as you have to think about what the best birthday present would be for a close friend, you have to think about how best to reach your clients. What works with their personalities?

## IT'S PARTY TIME . . . MAYBE

In general, you should be consultative on a regular basis, advises John Bowen. "Annual client appreciation dinners are okay. They're not necessary, but they are nice." But don't cross the line—your clients aren't your friends. "I'm not shopping for friends," says Bowen. "With a financial advisor, clients are looking to delegate responsibility. When I choose my CPA or lawyer, I'm not looking for social interaction. I want my problems solved. Frankly, I never go to my lawyer's client appreciation dates. It's a great business development tool—but what's in it for the client?"

Sharon Kayfetz worries that your appreciation dinner may be ill timed, especially if it's been a difficult year. "Are you giving clients the wrong message?" That is, do they look around and reflect that their fees are paying for this largesse? "Here's what's better to do for clients. Show them that you're cutting expenses in this market. Income is down. So don't shower gifts. You don't want them to think that maybe you're doing better than you are."

Still, properly planned, a social event can be an effective way of saying, "Thank you for your confidence and loyalty this past year." It doesn't have to be fancy. A casual open house suits Jeff Rattiner. "We have them once a year, and I think we probably need to do them more often." He keeps it simple: wine, cheese, hors d'oeuvres. "It's a good occasion for people to grab me for a one-on-one talk."

Other planners eschew dinners because they want to emphasize the unique natures of their clients. They entertain—but individually. "We surveyed our clients and asked them whether they wanted client appreciation dinners or for us to bring in speakers, and we got a lukewarm response," said Ross Levin. "We often buy a table at a charitable event, and then we'll bring *specific* clients to that. In the summer, we figure out which clients we're going to take golfing, for example. We try to do more individualized outings than a broad appreciation dinner. It's in keeping with our practice. We consider we have a highly individualized practice, where everyone who comes in is treated differently."

Another reason to entertain individually rather than en masse is privacy. You know all your clients, but they may not know who else is a client. This can be particularly awkward in a small community, where people who know each other in other contexts suddenly find they also share a financial advisor.

"We've had client appreciation dinners," says Deena Katz. "But we're very careful on how we do that, because clients are very concerned about confidentiality. We don't have a big free-for-all. We're having a big dinner next month, with an editor of Barron's coming for a talk." She tells the clients that other clients will be there, so if they want to keep the relationship private, she will understand if they don't want to come. "Some love to see each other; they know each other and love to come and have a good time. But we make it very clear what we're doing and why we're doing it."

Katz has also taken out some clients by themselves, and she keeps careful track of how often the firm has reached out to each client. "We have a scheduled touch routine. How many times did they get called? How many times did they get mailed? Get taken to dinner? Or go out, or whatever?" It's a planned casualness: "To us, it's very structured, but to the client it seems very natural."

Confidentiality also concerns Amy Leavitt. "I took the attitude that I would be very confidential with clients. In Vermont, I found, people actually like going out of town to a financial planner to preserve their privacy. So I've been very guarded." So for her practice, any kind of dinner or open house was out of the question. "I just serviced them to death to show my appreciation. Sometimes I've handed out tickets to sporting events or taken individual clients out to dinner—touches like that."

But, if you do individual events, warns Armstrong, be fair. "Don't give any client a reason to think you are favoring others more."

## THE LOW-KEY COMMUNICATOR

Of course, you can keep close to your clients without involving shrimp cocktails. Sometimes the simplest ways are the most effective. Ron Simons, the CPA who has handled my taxes since my first full-time job, sends me a letter every December thanking me for my continued business, reminding me of his services, and letting me know it'll soon be time to take care of my taxes again. The real estate agent who sold us our house sends us a card on the anniversary of our closing every year. His feeling is: once a client, always a client.

All planners do something to keep in touch with their clients, but what they do can vary greatly. As a rule of thumb, those with relatively few high net-worth clients stay in closer touch by phone, e-mail, and in-person interviews than those with a longer list of middle-income clients. But this doesn't mean that the well-off want to be overwhelmed with material. Again, you have to consider your client list.

"We manage our clients' expectations," says Katz. "You can't possibly do that unless you know what they are. So we ask them in the beginning, how do you want to be connected? How often? Do you prefer e-mail or snail mail? We get a good idea of how they want us to be involved in their daily lives." The firm learned this lesson the hard way, she says. "For example, we'd clip articles that we thought might interest our doctor clients and send them off. But some of them said to us, 'I don't need to see all this stuff. You're sending me too much stuff. I don't have time to read it.' Just because you think it's of value, doesn't mean your client does." So you have to ask them—what do they want to get? "Because there are some who have more time than God, and they'll be real happy to get whatever you send."

Katz's firm, Evensky, Brown and Katz, has one of my favorite reach-out tools—a *blog*. Short for Web log, these online diaries are mostly of use to in-the-know Web surfers. But firm partner Harold Evensky has started one on his Web site. An August 2003 posting discussed a problem of style drift under the title, "Buy a Banana, Own a Pickle." The same month, he also shared some thoughts on a presentation he'd attended at a financial planning conference, including how the speaker's ideas have affected the way he approaches his practice.

No matter what you do, you have to be proactive, says Stana-solovich, especially for the typical high-end client. "Our clients get called at least monthly to schedule an appointment for a meeting." This contact is in addition to specific requests for a meeting to discuss a particular problem or issue. "These points of contact create more opportunities for the advisors to do more in-depth work. For example, we send out tons of letters to clients about quarterly estimates, up-to-date tax projections, and things like that."

You can sign up for one of Stanasolovich's newsletters on his Web site. He offers specific products for different clients: businesses, individuals and families, medical doctors, tech professionals, and retirees.

In a client's first year with the firm, Levin is especially solicitous, meeting with them six times a year. "After the first year, depending on how complex the client's needs are, we have two to four face-to-face meetings a year. We do quarterly investment rebalancing and quarterly investment reporting." His firm's database provides other points of contact. "We can screen for clients with mortgages that are higher than a certain rate and call them and say, you know, you really should refinance." No client is going to feel overwhelmed with that kind of call.

Because Levin does not accept discretion on investment accounts, he has to keep in close touch with clients on investment decisions. Today, this contact is done mostly by e-mail, although Levin says there is a struggle for balance. "Our contention is that phone calls are much better than e-mails—they're more personal, people appreciate them more and remember them more. But e-mails are far more efficient. So we e-mail *tactical* things, but we also try to make phone calls." For a more personal touch, he sends cards if a client is in a hospital, and he remembers wedding anniversaries. "We try to stay tightly involved with our clients."

Dan Moisand, however, doesn't want to stay *too* close to his clients. Like Katz, he worries about overwhelming them. "We will call clients periodically, and as far as a meeting schedule goes, we'll let them dictate that to a degree. We want to see them at least once a year. But we don't force them to come in quarterly. It's a philosophy that a great deal of our value comes from the delegation function. Their time and energy is freed so they can pursue higher-purpose activities—things they can't delegate. So to drag them in, when they're not too inclined to do so, when we're communicating regularly, doesn't make sense."

This regular communication includes a quarterly mini-newsletter that gets sent with the quarterly reports. "We talk about a number of topics, none of them in a lot of depth. In between, one or twice, we also send out intraquarter commentary, where we go into an issue in some depth." For example, last year he issued some commentary on the war's effects on the market. Other issues talked about bonds and how to manage risk in a bond portfolio and tax code changes. These generally go by e-mail, but keeping in mind that different clients like different delivery systems, he sends hard copies to the few who still prefer paper. "So it's hard copy reports once a quarter and at least something via e-mail or a hard copy virtually every month."

These written and phone communications can be scaled up as your firm grows, as Ric Edelman shows. After the initial meetings, "It's a matter of ongoing service—typically done over the phone. There are periodic client review meetings, typically once a year, maybe more depending on client need. And we have massive amounts of client communication. Clients hear from us, one way or another, generally, two to five times a month." Edelman sends a monthly newsletter and a weekly online newsletter in addition to more personal phone calls or e-mails from the individual advisors. He also stages client-only seminars.

Edelman charges for his newsletter—which is unusual. Most planners see them as client outreach or marketing tools, but a few have managed to make them pay. (Ed Slott, whose newsletter is aimed mostly at other professionals, also charges for his publication.) However, Edelman gives a money-back guarantee—cancel the subscription anytime, get a full refund, and keep any issues you received meanwhile for free.

## DO IT YOURSELF?

As noted previously, most planners don't have the time or resources to prepare elaborate newsletters. However, as shown in the Resources, privately branded newsletters are available. Many planners in this book use the news written by Advisor-Sites, the company that built their Web sites. A broker-dealer or insurance company with which you are affiliated may have generic newsletters you can send out over your name, and you may find you have time for occasional writing yourself. For example, Morris Armstrong found time for an article on his specialty, divorce planning. He has posted it on his Web site: "Some Financial Hints for Divorce." A middle-ground option between total outsourcing and doing it yourself is hiring your own freelance writer essentially to interview you and turn your notes into articles and newsletters. Resources for various services are in the back of this book.

For an example of a perfectly designed and formatted newsletter, sign up for John Bowen's *Elite Advisor.* It's aimed at professionals, but it's a masterpiece of how to present just enough information to help readers without overwhelming them. It's in what is called *HTML format*—meaning that it looks like a Web page, with various fonts and colors. Again, as shown in the Resources, simple programs will let you easily design print or electronic newsletters, even if you're not a computer expert.

In fact, if you have the time, you can do your own print newsletter, in all or in part. You can write it and design it, too, and outsource the printing to Kinko's or a similar operation. Planners who write their own copy should follow some key rules, however.

- *Keep it simple.* Write what you know about. This is not a time to show off. To-the-point articles about a new tax regulation and how it will affect your clients will do the trick, or they can be explanatory—what is the dividing line between small-cap and large-cap? What is the difference between a growth stock and a value stock? How do the Fed changes affect portfolios—if they do at all?
- *Get someone to proofread your copy.* No writers can check their own material. Have an employee read your mate-

rial, or your spouse, or your English major daughter, or your neighbor. Nothing looks less professional than copy with typos.

- *Feel free to share.* Ed Slott's newsletter has a guest columnist. So, if your clients are interested in trusts, maybe you can find a trust lawyer in your town through the bar association who will write an article or let you do an interview. You're making the lawyer look good and possibly driving business their way, so you're doing each other a favor.

- *Remember that you are not the art director of* Vogue. Simple design and layout programs, as noted in the Resources, let even the most visually challenged design a client newsletter, but don't get complicated. A simple design is best. Discipline yourself and use only two fonts: Arial is great for headlines, and Times New Roman works nicely for text.

- *Keep it short.* Don't overwhelm yourself. A ledger-size page (11″ × 17″) gives you four 8½″ × 11″ pages to fill. It can be sent neatly with other mailings to your clients.

If you send an e-mail newsletter, the rules are pretty much the same. As noted above, you can send it in an HTML format. However, if you are not comfortable designing this material, you're probably better off just sending your clients an electronic version of your print newsletter. You can save it as a Word or PDF document and send it as an attachment.

Microsoft Outlook and other e-mail programs let you keep multiple address books with your clients' e-mail addresses. Do not just add all your clients' e-mail addresses into the To box however. This will let every client see the e-mail addresses of every other client. Most e-mail programs let you create an address group called Valued Clients or whatever. It keeps all e-mail addresses private. Alternatively, you can put your own e-mail in the To box and every other e-mail into the BCC (blind carbon copy) box. This approach also will hide all other addresses.

# THE DENTIST MODEL

In Chapter 3, I discussed the differences between serving delegators and serving validators. Delegators pretty much want you to do everything and just report back periodically. Validators take a lot of responsibility for their own financial affairs. The kind of clientele you have will affect how you stay in touch.

Several planners spoke of sending postcards, reminding clients to stay in touch. Instead of reaching out to their clients, they invite their clients to call them with any issues and to make appointments for periodic plan updates or portfolio rebalancings. Several used the metaphor of a dental office. Chances are, your dentist reminds you every six months that it's time for a checkup and a cleaning. The dentist doesn't call and nag you to come in or send you articles about dental health. He or she doesn't call you weekly to make sure you're flossing and have stopped eating peanut brittle. These planners say, "We're here. If you want more contact, give us a call."

"For example," says Amy Leavitt, "we send a letter to a client in January saying we will call in July—is that a good time? We build a lot around the annual plan updates. That sets out the course for how we're going to deal with the rest of the year. We encourage clients to phone, because we don't call to say, 'How are you doing?' other than those times." She tells them upfront that's not the way the firm works—but if a client wants to pick up the phone, she's there. "Basically, they pay for a year's worth of service, so we want them to use us. That assistance does not increase their bill." Recently, she's started sending newsletters and e-mails customized for different kinds of clients.

"We never make a proactive phone call," says Sheryl Garrett. "We're really clear up front so they don't have any illusions that we're going to call them. Of course, if they call us, we call them back. It's like a dentist's office—you schedule your next appointment on the way out of the checkup, and you don't hear from us meanwhile." But if there is a financial "toothache," you can call.

Of course, with Garrett's hourly model, extensive reaching out is not part of the deal. There are no freebies. "We charge $3 a minute in six-minute increments, so if we picked up a phone and called, we'd have to charge them, and they won't be happy about that unless it was critical. After all, they didn't authorize it."

However, even in this model it is possible, and even necessary, to keep in touch in a general way. Garrett communicates with clients two to three times a year by e-mail or regular mail. "For example, in early December we sent a holiday letter—a kind of an update. Did someone have a baby? Is there a new staffer? What's Sheryl up to? We thank them for their referrals and give them a password to the site."

For efficient, cost-effective e-mail, she relies on her Web-based system (set up through AdvisorSites—see Chapter 2, "Bits and Bytes.") "I put the letter on the site and then I can actually push it to various lists on an automated basis. We'll be doing this going forward." When the markets were in particularly bad shape, everyone asked her what she was thinking. "We heard a lot from clients, so we put together an official corporate communication to all clients. We posted it in the public portion of the site as well, because it was important for everyone to know what we were thinking. We wanted to indicate that we were in this for a long haul, to keep an eye on grand prize, and if it's been a while since a checkup, it's time for a review." She also puts out occasional current events newsletters, like after 9/11, to let her clients know she is thinking of them. "We got a lot of wonderful feedback. These types of outreach—if they don't come constantly—are helpful. They actually read it."

So like so many other advisors, no matter what their model, she is cautious about overwhelming her clients. "I'm a little leery of using a push service where they might get something weekly or even monthly. But possibly quarterly. But I really think a couple times a year for our kind of client is a must. A lot of good mileage to stay on person's consciousness. But not too much, or they start ignoring them. We only send something if we have something to say. If there's something specific, they need an appointment."

She encourages the planners in her network to send a post-card to clients to schedule a checkup. "It's been six months or a year—call to schedule. We pretty much want it at least annually. I want to encourage them to maintain regular contact. One fellow had a quick question, and we probably communicate two to three times a year, but we do a face-to-face only every two years, for an actual thorough review. It's a pretty good frequency, because we are staying in touch."

# GO WITH YOUR INSTINCTS

As I looked over all the responses I got for reaching out, I realized how hard it was to draw a conclusion. In this chapter, I've tried to present some of the many ways to reach out. What is right for your practice? You have to look at who your clients are. High net-worth clients are busy but may expect a lot of personal attention. Retirees have a lot of time. You, of course, give personal attention to all your clients, but it may not be practical to give every member of a large group of middle-income clients the same hand-holding as you do with a small group of wealthy clients. Nor may this be even necessary. Consider the possibilities and trust your instincts.

C *a s e* S *t u d y*
## KEEP THEM DOWN ON THE FARM

Katie Spenser, the planner from Chapter 6 who moved to her vacation town to establish a practice for teachers and small business owners, has been successful so far. She has landed clients in both niches. But, just as these people are different from the clients she knew in Boston, communicating with them is also different. Some of them have lived their whole lives in a rural environment, while others moved there with for the express purpose of living a rural lifestyle. Some have embraced high-speed technology (which, ironically, has often made their small town residence possible), while others are more traditional.

She'll have to adjust her communicating skills accordingly.

For example, Katie considered, then dropped, the idea of firm mixer. In the city, her firm had a huge holiday party for clients, and most of them came. Some of the clients knew each other already, because they had been the source for referrals, their kids went to the same prep schools, or they belonged to the same clubs. But Boston was a big city, and there was little embarrassment when they ran into each other. There wasn't a lot of, "Oh, I didn't know *you* were a client," and the minority who valued their privacy more intensely just didn't come.

But it's likely that most of Katie's clients know each other, and a party may not be a good idea. The small town atmosphere may be a little too close. Katie—but no one else—knows that two of her clients are bitter rivals for a seat on the town council. They would not thank Katie for bringing them together at a client event. In the end, she might have mostly no-shows.

But with the holiday season approaching, she can still do one-on-one events. She calls Donna and Ed, who own the printing company and employ 25. "Donna—it's Katie Spenser, your financial planner. I hope you and Ed are well. We met just last month, and I don't see a need to go over your financial status right now. However, you're one of my top clients, and I'd like to take you and Ed out to dinner sometime this month. This isn't really a business event—I don't want to make this an occasion to discuss your portfolio or any new products. But this could be a good opportunity to discuss any general issues about how we work together that *you* would like to bring up. And it's a thank you for all your business."

Donna and Ed are pleasantly surprised. They take out customers but are rarely taken out themselves. If this works well, Katie plans to make dinner a regular event for all of her top clients. The tone is casual, but she plans to keep careful track of whom she takes out when—no client should feel slighted.

However, Katie knows dinners aren't going to replace more formal communication, and she has to tailor that to each client. Donna and Ed live for e-mail. When Katie signed them on, they said, "Communicate with us as often as you feel necessary, but do it by e-mail. That's the easiest way for us." Both of them have PDAs and download each day's e-mail for review after the kids have gone to sleep. They answer and file replies the next morning, when they synch the handheld devices with the desktop machines in their office. Donna and Ed feel the strength in their business has come from watching the nickels and dimes, so they appreciate any updates Katie wants to send their way.

This approach contrasts with that of Nora and Phil. She is the assistant principal at the regional high school, and he's director of purchasing for the county. They have three school-aged children. "Frankly," said Phil, "the last thing we need is more stuff in our mail box, or e-mail box for that matter. Quarterly updates work fine for us."

"We hired you to make our lives simpler," stresses Nora. "We like that you're keeping an eye on our IRAs, on my 403(b), on the children's 529 plans. And we're happy with the way you're taking care of the inheritance I got from my mother. In short, don't tell us more than we need to know."

But Thomas thinks he needs to know a lot. He owns a steak house in town. He's a widower and pretty much retired, leaving the running of the restaurant to his chef son and manager daughter-in-law. Both generations are clients of Katie's. The son, Junior, and daughter-in-law, Janice, are easygoing, but Thomas has a lot of time on his hands and wants constant updates on his portfolio. "Is it up this month? How's my IRA? Should I be worried? Remember we discussed the process of transferring ownership to the kids—should we accelerate that now or slow it down?"

"You know," she says, "if you like the idea, I could send you a monthly snapshot of where you are, with the understanding that we aren't going to make major changes more than once or twice a year, as conditions change. Would you like that? I know you don't like e-mail, so I'll just slip it into an envelope and mail it to you. How would that work?" Actually, it worked well, because Thomas's real concern is that Katie is not paying attention to his account. A monthly mailing allays these fears.

"I'm glad you're keeping Dad happy," says Junior. "But running a kitchen, two meals a day, six days a week, keeps me busy enough. Once a quarter is fine for us, and we don't see a need for me and Janice to meet with you more than once a year."

At the other extreme from Thomas is Sandra, a young, single teacher whose finances are no more complicated than a 403(b) allocation. "Katie, I seem to have 30 choices here. My brother-in-law says Asia is poised to take off and I should have everything in international funds. My father says you can't go wrong with bonds. What do I do?" After talking with Sandra about her status and long-term plans, Katie advises her on an allocation. "Your situation is fairly simple," says Katie. "I don't think we have to meet again for a while. Of course, if there's a life change, like marriage or a home purchase, we can go over your situation again. However, we can meet again next year to look again at this allocation. Why don't I just make a note and get in touch with you again next year?" Sandra loves this solution—no complicated performance reports to look at but the knowledge a professional has a handle on her retirement fund.

In her contact manager program, Katie makes careful notes on how everyone wants to be contacted, and when. Communication can get complex, but it keeps everyone happy.

Meanwhile, Katie plans one mailing that every client will get—a short newsletter that she can either print and put in an envelope or e-mail as an attachment. To start, she is going to limit it to once a quarter, when most of her clients get quarterly statements anyway. It won't be long or complicated—a couple of items about the new tax law, or perhaps an explanation of how Roth IRAs work and how they differ from regular IRAs.

To show she is a member of the community, she will also add at least one item about a local situation—how property taxes are calculated, for example, or what the new state budget might mean for their county.

She is going to keep production simple. Although Adobe makes an excellent, affordable design tool for creating documents in the popular PDF format, Katie wants to start small and use what she has. Microsoft Word can serve as a good, basic layout program, easily converting text into columns for a professional look. With the addition of some clip art, it's a short, friendly, financial newsletter.

It's also a great deal of work. As her practice continues to grow, Katie wonders if she will have time to write her own copy, do all the fact checking, and carefully proofread. Although she has the time now, she may purchase client newsletters in the future, perhaps adding only the local piece, which she will continue to write herself. In the meantime, for the next quarter, she may enlist other professionals, like a local CPA who can contribute "Top Ten Year-End Tax Planning Tips" in exchange for the free publicity.

But perhaps the biggest outreach is what happens every day. Katie can recognize any of her clients when she sees them on the street, and this happens often in a small town. She runs into them at the post office, the supermarket, and the Fourth of July parade. "How are you doing? How are your children? Did you catch anything on last week's fishing trip?" As she continues to customize her outreach efforts and build on casual contacts, Katie finds clients becoming friends and friends becoming clients—the lines continuing to blur over time.

# EXECUTIVE SUMMARY

- Reaching out to clients and making sure they know that you are thinking of them is essential.
- Outreach can be done with e-mails, phone calls, newsletters, one-on-one thank-you dinners, or elaborate or casual group events.
- If you do a group event, it requires great care: don't be too lavish in a down year, and don't confuse a business thank-you with a pure social event.
- Understand that some clients prefer privacy and don't want to attend group events.
- One-on-one events are time consuming but are appreciated by wealthy clients—but be careful not to be seen as playing favorites.
- For phone, e-mail, and regular mail outreach efforts, consider who your clients are and ask them how often they want to be contacted. Some like lots of handholding, while others are busy and don't want to be bothered.
- If you have validator clients, you will likely want to stick with simple, occasional mailings in addition to regular client meetings.
- Newsletters can be outsourced through various services and freelancers.
- Ultimately, you have to tailor your outreach efforts to your clientele.

# 7

# DOING WELL
# BY DOING GOOD

**W**hen I was working at the *Journal of Accountancy*, I got a call from a professor of accounting. He asked how he could get permission to make about 30 photocopies of an article from the magazine for his students and how much we charge. I thanked him for his honesty and said I'd check, but I thought it would be little or no money. "But you know," I said, "I hear anecdotally that instructors do this all the time and never even go through the formality of asking permission."

"Well," replied the professor, "to be perfectly honest, I used to make photocopies myself without asking permission, but for this course, I thought I'd better ask. It's a course on business ethics."

This was long before Arthur Andersen imploded, before Enron, WorldCom, and arguments over B shares. This joke may be poignant now, but it was funny then, because the ethical bona fides of a CPA were beyond question. Fortunately, the accounting profession doesn't seem to have been permanently damaged by the actions of a few, and the large number of small practitioners who provide tax, accounting, and financial planning services retain the high reputation they deserve.

However, recent ethical disasters hold a lesson for the financial services industry generally, including financial planners. The smallest actions of even a few people can hurt an entire profession. It goes without saying that your actions have to be completely ethical, but beyond that, they have to be perceived as ethical. It's been a principle of CPAs for years that even the appearance of unethical behavior is wrong, and smart financial planners have followed that principle, too.

A treatise on ethical behavior is beyond the scope of this book, but I will look at it from a practice management viewpoint. In tough times, especially, when people are nervous and newspapers reveal a new scandal every week, the perception of ethical behavior becomes essential to your practice. Unless potential clients see you as ethical, you won't get any further. I'm using ethical in a wide sense here: not only honest with clients' money but honest about your competency—honest about your ability to handle your clients' needs.

You can't say, "I'm ethical," says John Bowen. "Judging your character is the only way. Some advisors try to tell clients how great they are, but this doesn't work. Don't spend time saying how great you are. Instead, ask really good questions." In fact, Bowen suggests you tape yourself so you can see how you come across. Do you come across as engaged? "You are judged by the quality of your questions." In brief, says Bowen, follow what he calls the Mom Rule: "Treat every client like your mother."

## WHAT COMPENSATION SAYS . . . AND DOESN'T SAY

As I noted in Chapter 3, the profession is facing a big schism between those planners who charge only fees and those who get some or all of their income from commissions. You have to consider what model best suits your clients as well as your own preferences. There isn't an ethics difference, however. Nothing about selling products makes you unethical.

However, there is a *perception* issue. Planners who work at least partly on commission have to deal with the suspicion on the part of many prospective clients that they are "just salespeople." However, this doesn't have to be a problem. The key is to be upfront from the beginning, exercising full disclosure, as Amy Leavitt does.

"Trust is the core. It is everything, and in our initial interview, we explain what we do, and we make full disclosure as far as who we are, how we get paid, and what the SEC rules are regarding testimonials." Within the bounds of confidentiality, she says she tries to be as transparent about the firm as possible.

Great references also help with perception. "Top attorneys and accountants in the state know us. We have professional references and client references, and that's what we feel is the best way to do things." She even asks current clients, "How do we compare trustwise with other professionals? How do you know? What gave you the most confidence?" She uses clients as a personal focus group.

Alan Kahn is a CPA and a financial planner who derives some of his income from commissions. But he doesn't let that affect him. "Never think about commissions," he advises. "Never think about how much you are going to make, because, over the long run, you will make money if you do the right thing. That's very, very important. Many people come to my office, and I sit with them and recommend things for them to do—things that I'm not going to make any money on. The clients turn around and ask me about this." That is, they want to know how I will earn money from these recommendations. "And I say, don't worry about that. If you're happy, you'll establish a long-term relationship with me, you'll stay with me, and where there is a need for a financial product, you'll buy it through me."

John Keeble, who was one of the founders of what became the financial planning profession some 40 years ago, had a commission-based practice and continues to speak about the importance of this model. Ric Edelman also works on commissions but, like Kahn, has not focused on this as the essence of his practice. "We build our business on education," he said, referring in particular to his early days of building the practice on free seminars.

But it can't be denied that fee-only advisors have less trouble describing their practice. Said Katz, "We take fiduciary responsibility, and we tell them so. We actually say, 'I am your fiduciary. I will act in your best interest at all times.' A lot of people don't. Brokers cannot make that statement, I explain. They act as an agent of their company. It's important for prospective clients at the outset to know what my responsibility for the engagement is."

Armstrong stresses his membership in NAPFA. Although it's a small group when compared with the FPA, for example, it has gotten a lot of press. Many consumers' publications and influential columnists have praised NAPFA, and the fee-only model generally, as being as pure as the driven snow—something Armstrong has realized. "So I do mention that I'm fee-only and that I belong to NAPFA." (In fact, he points out, compensation disclosure is required anyway.) "But I don't bash commission-based planning," he stresses, "I find that to be counterproductive." Of course, planners cannot join a group just because they think it's a marketing advantage. Armstrong emphasizes he truly believes in the fee-only model.

In fact, most of the commission bashing actually comes on behalf of fee-only planners rather than by them. Most of them will say something like, "I am fee-only because that's the way I like to practice and that's the way my clients like to compensate me." Armstrong says he does not think that NAPFA members are necessarily any smarter or ethical than other people.

As Dan Moisand puts it, "Compensation structure does not dictate competence and ethics. You can be a bad or unethical fee-only planner. But I've found it's easier for clients to make the leap under the fee-only structure. It's simpler for them to grasp. I was competent and ethical before I was fee-only. But this eliminates more than just conflict of interest—it eliminates the seeds of doubt that can enter the client's mind. There's some real value in that."

However, planners getting most or all of their compensation from fees can face their own special credibility problems in falling markets. Whether they are charging hourly, with a flat fee, or with the traditional assets-under-management arrangement, they may find a particular problem sending invoices out as the value of a portfolio falls. As one planner put it, "If the market is down 5 percent and your client's portfolio is down 3 percent, don't expect a thank-you."

Once again, the problem is one of perception—that you are collecting fees even if the market is down, even though you've done a competent, even exemplary, job. Some clients have called for various contingency models—the planner only makes money if the client makes money. There are various practical and regulatory problems with this, but at least one investment advisor has created a win together/lose together model.

Jeffrey Dunham, of Dunham & Associates in San Diego, manages $295 million in a range of proprietary investment vehicles and changes his compensation based on his performance. Like Katz, he says that clients want accountability. If one of his proprietary stock funds doesn't beat the agreed-upon benchmark index, the subadvisor will charge 25 basis points. But if the subadvisor outperforms the index, the fee could be 20 percent of the amount over the index. So in good years, everyone—advisors and clients—makes more.

The ultimate point is that any model has its advantages and its perceptual problems—but no one model has a monopoly on ethics.

# LETTERS AFTER YOUR NAME

No matter how you practice, however, credentials can help before you even shake hands with prospective clients. "People like the credentials I have," said Morris Armstrong. He has a CFP and ChFC designations and is also a certified divorce planner. "When I'm talking with a prospective client, I also mention that I am studying for the CFA designation and taking the test. They appreciate that." Deena Katz also finds that prospective clients appreciate the power of a designation.

"First of all, I'm a CFP, which has a code of ethics," she says, "and I tell the clients that. I explain it. I explain what I need to do to keep my license, to keep my certification. If I don't do that, it can be taken away. So that has some bite to it." That is, if she violates the ethics code, it's not just a "so what" situation. "I find it's important to note that I am bound by a code of ethics." Clients like to know what their recourse is if there's a problem. "People are looking for accountability."

With designations, we run into perceptions again. The CFP and CPA designations are well known among the general public, and everyone knows about law degrees and what *J.D.* means after a name. Other designations may be less well known. You shouldn't avoid them—some of them mandate a certain level of education that can only help your practice, if you want to focus on a certain area. However, don't expect current or prospective clients to have heard or even to care about some of the more obscure designations. Their value in establishing your competency or honesty may be minimal. (A list of designations can be found in the Resources.)

Institutions that offer financial services education, often leading toward a designation, have ethics courses. For example, the American College in Bryn Mawr, Pennsylvania, has such classes as ethics and human values, piecing together the ethical puzzle, and charting an ethical course of the multiline agent. The College for Financial Planning in Greenwood Village, Colorado, in addition to its certification programs, has a business ethics course as part of its Masters in Personal Financial Planning program.

## BEING GOOD AND LOOKING GOOD

There are other ways to come across as a capable and honest planner. Armstrong says he hasn't had a perceptual problem. "Maybe it's my age—I'm a little older, I'm not a 25-year-old." Also, he says, he has a good Web site, and right or wrong, "People seem to believe what they read on the Web. I have my background on it. If you do a name search, I pop up, with quotes about me from other people."

Like Bowen, Moisand says you can't just go out there say you're ethical. "This sounds corny, but my grandfather said a long time ago that for people to trust you, two conditions must exist. One, you must be trustworthy; two, don't expect anyone to believe a thing you have to say. I don't spend a whole lot of time trying to convince someone that I'm ethical." That is, a liar by definition can't tell you that they're a liar. Everyone will say that they're good and ethical. So he doesn't spend a lot of time saying, "Trust me." "But what you can do is provide little glimpses of evidence that allude to that. And the more third-party involvement, the better. So when someone asks me if I have a clean ethical record, I say, yes, and here's how to verify that: check CRD, IARD—the paper trail." Moisand's record is clean, but many investors have discovered records on other advisors that made them uncomfortable.

"When you're trying to convey that you're competent, instead of saying you're really good at what you do, I point to *Worth* and *Financial Planning*." Moisand has been singled out as a top planner in both publications. "They're people who know a good planner when they see one, and they say nice things about me."

Alan Kahn has paid particular attention to how ethics fits into his practice. One reason for his deep thoughtfulness may be his background as a CPA. Many of the past ethics rules for the accounting profession, like rules against advertising, look dated now but were written by practitioners who were concerned about their perception.

"Ethics is the most important question. Ethics and integrity, to me, are the most important things you can have and promulgate in your practice. I say that because a lot of people in our industry do unethical things. They give brokers a bad name, they give insurance people a bad time, they give financial planners a bad name. I always say, if you always do the right thing for people, you can never go wrong. It will always come back to you." You have to do what is right for the client. You can charge a commission or charge for the plan—but you can't look for the quick hit.

When he got started in financial planning some 20 years ago and was being trained, Kahn remembers being told that, "I had to make the sale immediately. And I'd say, if I just met the person, how can I expect to close a sale on the first or second meeting? That's not the type of client I was sitting down with. They said that I'd never survive in this business, because I needed to make a sale right away. And those people trying to make the quick sale on the first or the second meeting, they're all gone."

If your practice is long-term and you run it like a CPA, an attorney, or any professional out there, you have to look to investing in yourself, says Kahn. You are investing in your future. If you run an ethical practice, "Your people will become your gold mines. They will refer to you and bring you business just because you have always done the right thing."

This is true, he continues, whether you're a financial planner, CPA, attorney, executive—anything. "Too often today, if you're a business owner, loyalty and integrity go out the window. They just don't exist. People will change brokers, doctors, by the flip of a coin." Ethics is bound up in working together over a long term.

"For example, I've had a gardener for over 20 years. He's an old man, he works with a few people. So many people come to me and say they'll do my lawn for less money, and I say I'm not interested. I've been dealing with this guy for 20 years. And whatever needs to be done, he does." Neighbors have even given Kahn references to lower-priced gardeners who promise to do the same work. "But there is tremendous value in knowing somebody and working with them for a long time. Yes, you want value, you want the right products, the right service, but I think it's important to have that loyalty, which a lot of people just don't consider valuable any more."

Most of Kahn's clients have been with the firm for many years. "In fact, I tell them, once you start with us, you're stuck with us forever—unless you *want* to leave. That's very important. If anyone asks what's the key to being a successful anything, it's having integrity and loyalty. And being honest with yourself and clients. You have to let them know you're more concerned about them than yourself. And I always treat someone's money, insurance—anything we handle for a client—we always treat like it was our own. And that, to me, is very important. And when I handle someone's money, I tell them don't worry about it—I'll be worrying about it for you!"

## WORKING IN THE COMMUNITY

Coming across as an upright planner can also be a matter of coming across as an upright neighbor. How are you viewed by the people in the town where you practice? I live a few blocks from some Little League fields, and the fence is ringed with banners of local businesses who support the teams. That sends a message to all the parents who come out to cheer on their kids. As a marketing or advertising tool, this is very limited, but it does set a tone for your practice.

Dan Moisand has supported local events like this, and members of Lou Stanasolovich's firm helped set up a playground specially designed for physically and mentally challenged children. Ross Levin and his firm have done charitable work. Ric Edelman serves on the board of directors of the United Way of the National Capital Area, Junior Achievement of the National Capital Area, and the Boys and Girls Clubs of Greater Washington.

Volunteerism can really buff your image, but it has to be honest. That is, if you are just into it to impress potential clients, they will realize your true motivations quickly. As movie czar Samuel Goldwyn allegedly said, "Sincerity is the most important thing in making movies. If you can fake that, you've got it made."

As noted in Chapter 6, "Schmooze or Lose," seminars for nonprofit groups are welcome. Give a talk to a business owner's group on the state of the economy. If tax prep is part of your practice, you can provide assistance for the elderly or others who can't easily afford advice.

Many professional organizations have formal assistance programs to encourage planners to give back. Recently, the San Francisco chapter of the FPA actually modified its bylaws to encourage planners to donate some time for the public good. Kacy Gott, the chapter's chair, was quoted as saying, "We believe that it's the responsibility of the members to give back." David Yeske, president of the FPA, said, "By and large, it seems like most of our members have this fairly strong desire to be giving back to society and perform some sort of public service. This is going to be a model for a lot of other chapters."

Ethics permeates the work with your town, your employees, and both current and prospective clients. In this chapter, I can only provide advice on perception. On actually running a clean practice, you have to count on yourself. "You can't teach ethics, just like you can't teach someone to be something they're not," says Kahn. "Ethics has to come from within. It comes from your roots."

# FROM THE TOP

Major financial groups have all weighed in on ethics—both on good behavior and the appearance of good behavior. Here are a few examples. These are by no means all-inclusive, and if you are subject, either by law or by membership, to the rules of these organizations, consult the group for the full, up-to-date rules. I'm excerpting some of them here to give you a sense of how widely ethics covers your practice. Consider especially Principle 1 from the FPA, which requires adherence to the *spirit* of the rules, not just the letter.

## Financial Planning Association

The FPA has a Code of Ethics, worth consideration whether or not you are a member. The Code has seven principles, adapted from the CFP Board.

1. *Integrity.* "An FPA member shall offer and provide professional services with integrity." "Integrity requires an FPA member to observe not only the letter but also the spirit of this Code."
2. *Objectivity.* "An FPA member shall be objective in providing professional services to clients."
3. *Competence.* "An FPA member shall provide services to clients competently and maintain the necessary knowledge and skill to continue to do so in those areas in which the designee is engaged."
4. *Fairness.* "An FPA member shall perform professional services in a manner that is fair and reasonable to clients,

principals, partners, and employers and shall disclose conflict(s) of interest(s) in providing such services."

5. *Confidentiality.* "An FPA member shall not disclose any confidential client information without the specific consent of the client unless in response to proper legal process, to defend against charges of wrongdoing by the FPA member, or in connection with a civil dispute between the FPA member and client."

6. *Professionalism.* "An FPA member's conduct in all matters shall reflect credit upon the profession."

7. *Diligence.* "An FPA member shall act diligently in providing professional services. Diligence is the provision of services in a reasonably prompt and thorough manner. Diligence also includes proper planning for and supervision of the rendering of professional services."

## American Institute of CPAs

The AICPA has provided a list of situations that could cause an ethical dilemma for a planner.

- Providing services for both members of a couple in the midst of a divorce
- Suggesting a client invest in a business in which you have a financial interest
- Providing services for several members of a family who may have opposing interests
- Serving on a community's tax board, which is handling issues that involve one of your clients
- You refer a client to an insurance broker or other service provider, which refers clients to you under an exclusive arrangement. (This actually may violate other organizations' rules and various laws, and even if it didn't, can you

imagine how furious a client would be upon finding out the basis of your recommendations?)

## CFP Board of Standards

This group, which oversees the CFP designation, goes into detail on ethics. Below are some brief selections of what I (and not necessary anyone at the Board) think are some of the most important rules.

- *Advertising.* "A CFP Board designee shall not make a false or misleading communication about the size, scope, or areas of competence of the CFP Board designee's practice. . . ."
- *Promotion.* "In promotional activities, a CFP Board designee shall not make materially false or misleading communications to the public or create unjustified expectations regarding matters relating to financial planning or the professional activities and competence of the CFP Board designee."
- *Keeping up.* "A CFP Board designee shall keep informed of developments in the field of financial planning and participate in continuing education throughout the CFP Board designee's professional career in order to improve professional competence in all areas in which the CFP Board designee is engaged."
- *Compensation.* "Disclose conflict(s) of interest and sources of compensation; and inform the client or prospective client of his/her right to ask at any time for information about the compensation of the CFP Board designee."
- *Respect.* "A CFP Board designee shall show respect for other financial planning professionals, and related occupational groups, by engaging in fair and honorable competitive practices."

## APPEARING TO BE GOOD

Haley Clemens, CFP, CPA/PFS, has a well-established, fee-only practice in Chicago. For some years, she has employed a paraplanner and an office manager. Slowly, but steadily, she has continued to add mostly high net-worth clients to her roster. In fact, in an effort to continue to provide top service, she recently hired a second professional for the firm, a young CFP. Zachary will work alongside Haley for a while and eventually take over some of the firm's clients himself.

On a practical level, this arrangement proceeds well. Even in his first week, Zachary shows himself to be a talented planner and eager to learn more. Even though it will take a while before his work actually pays off in increased revenue, Haley appreciates having more time to focus on long-term strategy—and she knows she'll be less nervous going on vacation if another professional planner is available to her clients.

However, the firm is running into *perceptual* problems, some of which are the unintended result of hiring Zachary and others the result of a national economic zeitgeist. In a rush one day to get to an appointment out the office, Haley gives Zachary the number of a client she plans to transition to him and tells him to call the client and introduce himself, after familiarizing himself with the client's file. "We'll go over the details on this guy later," she says, grabbing her coat and running out the door.

When she gets back, Zachary tells her he had a good talk with the client, a Mr. Horace. But on her way to her office, the office manager stops her and speaks to her quietly. "Mr. Horace just called and said he wanted to speak to you—and just to you, Haley. He sounded very insistent." Wondering what Zachary did to upset Mr. Horace, she quickly calls him.

"Ms. Clemens? Thanks for getting back to me so quickly. I appreciate it. You know, I just spoke to your new associate. He sounds like a nice boy," Mr. Horace is probably old enough to be Zachary's grandfather, "but you know, you and I have been working together for years, and I don't know if I want to start with someone new. Also, you have umpteen years of experience, and this kid—and I'm sure he's bright—sounds like the ink is still wet on his college diploma."

Haley spends the next half hour calming Mr. Horace. "I'm sorry you were under the impression that you were losing me, Mr. Horace. Actually, it's the exact opposite. My new associate, Zachary, will be working with you to answer ongoing questions you have about your portfolio. As he familiarizes himself with your financial plan, he will increasingly be giving you investment advice. However, this is to free me to spend more time researching the mutual funds and managed accounts we use to serve you. Like me, Zachary is a Certified Financial Planner, which means that even before joining me he had to pass a major exam and meet some stringent experience requirements. Although he's young, he already has considerable knowledge and skills. And I will always be signing off on your annual rebalancings." She says, almost coining a phrase, "You aren't losing me, Mr. Horace, you are gaining Zachary."

He grumbles a little but eventually gives in, and she finally ends the call with Mr. Horace agreeing to see how it goes. "Right speech, but too late," Haley says to herself. She looks at the list she scribbled of the five clients she was going to start Zachary with. Before she gives him the other four phone numbers, she calls each one herself.

"George? It's Haley Clemens. Good to talk with you . . . no, there are no problems with your portfolio. In fact, things are going so well here, I've had occasion to add to my staff, and hired a new Certified Financial Planner. His name his Zachary, and I wanted to let you know so you won't be startled when he calls you. He and I will both be working with you in the future.

I've hired him so I can spend more time on intensive portfolio management tasks and product research—I want to make sure you and my other clients aren't missing out on anything that might be appropriate for your portfolios. In fact, can you join us for lunch in the next week or so to meet Zachary and go over your situation?"

"Haley, I'm so glad your business is doing so well you can expand—and I appreciate the heads up. I'm sure that if you hired Zachary, he must be good, and I'd love to meet him. Does Thursday at 12:30 PM work for you?"

Haley breathes a sigh of relief. George is usually even more difficult than Mr. Horace. He's a hard-driving corporate CEO and sensitive to any perceived slight. But, because Haley timed the speech before any changes actually happened, and because she emphasized the addition, not the change itself, he perceived Zachary's assignment to his portfolio as a plus, not a demotion on some sort of "client hierarchy." Haley starts to call the rest.

At 5:00 PM, she is seeing some new prospects—Mr. and Mrs. Williams, who were recommended by a current client. Of course, she will talk with them herself, but she asks Zachary to sit in so he can observe.

They are going to introduce an issue more problematic than a new employee. Financial scandals have tarred the entire financial profession, and Haley's prospects will put her on the defensive.

"Mr. and Mrs. Williams—I'm so glad Steve Wesley gave you my name. I want to hear about your financial situation and see if my firm can help you." She introduces her new associate. "If we decide we want to work together, I will be the one working with you primarily, but Zachary will be working with you as well."

"I have to tell you frankly, I'm nervous about this," says Mr. Williams. "I've always taken care of my finances myself, and I'm only here because, well, I got a really big promotion earlier this year which has given us a lot more money but a lot less time to manage it. Steve is an old college friend of mine, and he recommended you highly, and my wife—"

"—doesn't want to spend her spare time managing the money, either," says Mrs. Williams. "We trust Steve and think it's time we get some real professional advice with our finances."

"But I hear so many stories these days," continues Mr. Williams. "Enron, WorldCom—these sure looked like trustworthy companies. How do I know you're trustworthy?" He flushes a little. "No offense meant."

"None taken," says Haley. "Those are good questions. I can't *prove* I'm competent or ethical, but let me explain how I work and what kinds of oversight I have." Haley explains about Form ADV and what it means to be a registered investment advisor, under the authority of the SEC. "Zachary and I are both Certified Financial Planners. We have to meet continuing education requirements and obey an ethics code. If we fail, the CFP Board can discipline us or even take away our right to use the designation. You can check both of us online." In addition, Haley continues, she is a certified public accountant, supervised by the state board of accountancy. She is also a member of the American Institute of CPAs, which has a code of ethics, too.

"I see on your card that you are also a PFS," says Mrs. Williams. "I have heard of CFP and CPA, but not that one."

"It stands for Personal Financial Specialist. It's not as well known as CFP. It's a designation available only to planners who already are CPAs. It also has experience and education requirements. You can check out those on the AICPA Web site, just like you can check out the CFP requirements on the CFP Board Web site."

"About a year ago, before Steve gave me your name," says Mr. Williams, "I met some guy at the club who said he was a CFP, too, but then I found out he sold mutual funds, and I figured I don't need another salesperson in my life. Now Steve says you don't sell mutual funds . . ."

"Oh no," explodes Zachary, "we would *never* do that. We are completely fee-only—"

"Yes, that's right," says Haley, smoothly interrupting. "We don't sell on commission. We are not compensated for recommending a product, and we use no-load products. We make our money—and I will give you the exact details—as a percentage of assets under management. Sometimes we also work on an hourly basis, or annual retainer, based on a client's particular needs. However, many clients are more comfortable working with a planner who is mostly compensated by commissions on products they sell. For example, they may charge a flat fee for a plan, then earn commissions selling you products to implement it. In fact, that's the way this practice operated until we made a transition about five years ago." Many qualified planners continue to work that way, including CPAs and CFPs, she continues, and if that model suits them, she would be happy to give them some names—colleagues she knows from her FPA chapter.

"Well, I like the idea of just a fee," says Mr. Williams. "That's not a problem. But if we give you our money on an assets-under-management arrangement, and if our portfolio shrinks one year, I suppose we still have to keep paying you?"

"Yes, but you don't have to stay with me. I like to keep my clients in a plan for the long term—not just for a good quarter's performance. But if you become unhappy with me, you just pay me for work to date, and I will help you transfer your assets to another advisor. But I can't make you performance guarantees. And frankly, Mr. and Mrs. Williams, no honest financial advisor will give you a guaranteed return."

"Well, this guy on TV said he could guarantee. . . ." He goes on. Mrs. Williams rolls her eyes. Haley thinks, "Well, if you like the guy on TV, why the hell don't you give *him* your portfolio?"

"Mr. Williams, I am not familiar with that particular . . . personality. But I can only tell you that no true professional, whether working for commissions or fees, will make you a guarantee."

Mr. Williams shows a bit of a smile. "Well, maybe I need just a few more details then . . ."

At the end of the day, the Williams make an appointment for a follow-up visit. Mr. Williams even gives half an apology for giving Haley such a hard time. Mrs. Williams rolls her eyes again. After they leave, Haley and Zachary shut up the office and get their coats.

"Did you learn anything from that couple?" she asks with a wry smile.

"When I studied ethics while taking my CFP courses, I thought, 'Gee, it's easy being good.' But actually *looking* good—that's the hard part!"

---

# EXECUTIVE SUMMARY

- Ethical behavior, which includes a level of competency, is essential to the well-being of your practice.
- Ethics is not only about your behavior; it's about how others perceive you.
- You can't just state that you're ethical; you have to show integrity in how you run your practice.
- Compensation models do not make a planner either ethical or unethical. However, different models may present perceptual problems that have to be dealt with.
- Well-known designations offer a code of ethics and create a positive impression in the minds of consumers.
- Good works in the community raise your profile in the eyes of your neighbors.

Chapter

# 8

# THE UNIVERSITY OF LIFE

**A**t a technical accounting conference that I attended, one of the presenters was talking about his son, who had just become a CPA and joined his father in his practice. He said his son was complaining because the number of accounting standards had increased dramatically since the father had been in school. "My son said the CPA Exam was therefore harder for him than it was for me. All I could tell him was that in my day, the exam was still in Latin."

In English (or in English so convoluted it can read like Latin), the NASD, SEC, and various state agencies continue to churn out new regulations. Every year, the IRS has some regulatory innovation. If you're a CFP, CPA, or lawyer, all these professions have governing bodies that can redefine how you manage your practice. Keeping up can be tough. If you're affiliated with a broker-dealer, the compliance staff at the home office can help keep you on your toes, but you can't abdicate all responsibility for developments.

Even beyond keeping up with compliance issues is staying apprised of new trends in managing your practice and all the new insurance products and funds. Several years ago, I was at a conference, and during lunch, I asked the professionals at my table if they could explain this new college planning product I was hearing about—the 529 plan. No one knew anything beyond a few basic facts. So, as soon as I got home, I researched and wrote an article about it—in the hope that there wouldn't be any more confused planners at conference lunch tables.

## ON BEING A COMPLIANT PLANNER

This is one area where you don't want to experiment. Useless software? You can replace it. Incompetent assistants? You can fire them. But, if you screw up compliance, it could be the end of your career. It's always been an issue, but the disasters that involved Enron, WorldCom, and Arthur Andersen have put financial professionals under a brighter light than they have ever been under before.

You're in pretty good shape if you are affiliated with a broker-dealer. No, you're not lawsuit-proof, but you do have access to compliance officers at the home office who can serve as a great resource. When I've spoken with registered reps about why they like their broker-dealers, praise for the compliance department was probably listed as a reason more often than high payouts. Your broker-dealer will accept their responsibility in this area, even if it's with a heavy heart. "It used to be that fear of losing market share is what kept us up at night," said one broker-dealer executive. "Now, it's compliance worries."

But it can get a little trickier if you're an independent registered investment advisor. At one compliance seminar I attended, the presenter, a lawyer specializing in SEC registration issues, said he once received a panicky call from an RIA. "I found out that the SEC requires all RIAs to maintain five years of complaints." So what's the problem? "I've only been in a business for one year—how can I have five years of files?" By the time you've been through the registration wringer, you may be that insane, too.

Depending on how big you are, you will be under the supervision of a state authority or the SEC. Either way, you're pretty much on your own, and many—perhaps most—RIAs choose to outsource compliance issues. But again, even with the top consulting firms, this is not a 100 percent foolproof solution. Advisors still have to take personal responsibility for compliance. "Compliance is a big thing," says Morris Armstrong. "I attend seminars and talk to other advisors. I'm my own RIA, so I need to worry about Connecticut statutes."

At least three advisors I interviewed used National Regulatory Services, a one-stop shop for investment advisory and broker-dealer compliance consulting. "I work with NRS," says Nancy Langdon Jones. "They help me with my Investment Advisor Registration Depository requirements." Charles Schwab, one of her custodians, also sends out compliance advice. She also subscribes to a newsletter from consulting firm the Consortium <www.liftburden.com>, an excellent investment for any RIA.

Lou Stanasolovich is also an NRS customer. "We've always used them. It was probably one of the best outsourcing decisions we ever made. It lessens my need to spend time on the regulatory side—well worth the cost. For me to spend my time trying to re-word my ADV properly would be an enormous waste of time." Ross Levin, another NRS customer, engaged a Chicago law firm to perform another useful service—a mock audit. The firm essentially pretends to be an auditor and catches any mistakes before a true auditor does. NRS and other firms also offer this service.

Still, you may have to look around to find a firm that understands your particular practice and its compliance needs. Although the rules are the same for everyone, their effect can differ from firm to firm. "In the past few years, I've employed about three different firms to varying degrees of satisfaction," says Sheryl Garrett. "And, basically, it's been really expensive and not personalized. Some were impossible to work with or talk to—it was horrible. So I really feel sorry for most people out there trying to work through this. It seems overwhelming, and it's so easy to make mistakes." She has recently contracted with Nancy Johnson, of Strategic Compliance Concepts, for compliance coaching. "We're now outsourcing compliance in its entirety. She completely and intimately understands our practice and how it works."

Whomever you go with, be aware of the wide variety of services that are available for outsourcing. The following is a selection of what NRS, for example, offers:

**ADV Review Service.**

- Examine services, fees, sources of compensation, and possible conflicts of interest, and issue a report that includes sample and recommended disclosures.
- Complete revision of ADV—parts I and II.

**Advertising/Performance Review.**

- Examine advertising and marketing materials in print and online.
- Review performance data.
- Make recommendations for proper and appropriate procedures and disclosures.

**Compliance in a Box.** NRS bills this as "a reference and sample document system that enables investment advisors to have professionally prepared client documents, trading forms, compliance guides, and registration documents. . . ." Included are:

- *Client documents.* Client Suitability Form, Form ADV Acknowledgement, Form ADV Annual Letters

- *Compliance guides.* SEC Inspection Checklist, SEC Inspection Survival Guide, Insider Trading Policy, Soft Dollar Checklist
- *Personal trading.* Quarterly Trading Report; SEC, ICI, AIMR Report Summaries; SEC Rule Requirements
- *Solicitor agreements.* Model Solicitor Agreement, Solicitor's Disclosure Document, Cash Solicitation Rule

Other resources appear at the end of this book. The point is not to wait until you have a problem before calling in help. The best defense against a noncompliance charge is never to make a mistake, and for that, you should stick with professionals. Compliance is not a do-it-yourself project.

# BEING A KNOW-IT-ALL

The science and science fiction writer Isaac Asimov told an anecdote that illustrated even an expert's inability to know everything. One year, right after the Nobel Prize for chemistry had been announced, a clever reporter called Asimov for commentary—knowing that Asimov himself had a Ph.D. in chemistry. But, after a few moments of thought, a deeply embarrassed Asimov had to admit that he had never heard of the winner before and had no idea what his winning achievement was.

You are not going to know everything, either, but you can reduce the chances that your clients will call you with a question that leaves you stumped. "My brother-in-law tells me I should be in exchange-traded funds—why are there none in my portfolio?" or, "My employees have asked me to set up a SIMPLE plan—is that right for my business?"

As noted above, if you are affiliated with a broker-dealer, the home office can be a great resource. Amy Leavitt has found that, "My primary source has been my broker-dealer. For example, as soon as the tax act was passed, their attorneys put together a synopsis, a how-does-it-affect-you strategy." She supplements this with industry conferences and subscriptions to the main industry magazines.

"Read magazines," says John Bowen. "Conferences are good, too." But he really suggests a formal study group with other planners in your area. The trick is to find one at the right level. "Groucho Marx said he didn't want to belong to any club that had someone like him as a member. Do you want a group that has someone like you as a member?" But, if you can find a group of like-minded planners—perhaps through a local FPA chapter—a meeting three to four times a year can be very helpful. "You can arrange to bring in outside speakers." And, as you get more comfortable, the members of the group would share their financials with each other.

"You have to keep up on new products," says Armstrong. "Reading material is key, and the Web is great for this. Also, companies themselves will keep you up to date—once they get your name, they send you brochures and flyers." One midsized firm even invited wholesalers to address regular meetings of the firm. Yes, these are usually geared to the wholesaler's specific products. However, a good wholesaler can also discuss how these products can fit in with clients' portfolios.

Lou Stanasolovich also agrees that reading is key. "I probably read three e-mail newsletters from *Inc.* a week, and I go through about 100 to 150 publications a month. And with the Internet, you can easily discover what's going on, so *The Wall Street Journal* is less timely, and less necessary, on a daily basis than it used to be." He gives priority to articles on business technology and how businesses are run. *Inc.*'s free, online newsletters cover topics such as sales and customer service, leading your company, business solutions, and small business technology.

For Deena Katz, perhaps the best resource you can have is a partner. "Each of you is responsible for different things. Harold is the investment guru. He reads a lot of things and then passes on to me the 'Reader's Digest' version. I do the same thing with him in compliance and practice management and other issues which I think he should be apprised of, but he doesn't have to dig down deep and know every little thing."

Her system consists of big basket in her office where she throws her publications. Then she takes them home at night. "And that's what I do before I go to sleep—which is probably not the best thing! But you have to do it at night. During the day, it's CNN and CNBC." When she travels, she takes magazines with her—but not stuffed into an extra suitcase. "We scan in articles and assign them key words, so I can get back to them if there's something I want. So, if I'm going to do a talk on 529 plans, I have a whole file of things electronically that I can get to and figure out what I want to use. We keep a lot of information that way." (Scanning software, described in Chapter 2, "Bits and Bytes," usually comes even with low-priced scanners.)

Ross Levin is no exception to the reading mania—in fact, he schedules his reading. "You have to do a tremendous amount of reading. I schedule my week so that I have client meetings back to back on Wednesday and Thursday. Tuesday afternoons are prospect meetings. And Monday and Friday are cleanup and reading and writing days, and Tuesday mornings are kind of cleanup and reading days." It's a matter of intensity, he says. "My client meetings are high intensity events. So I find it easier if I'm kind of in that mode, one right after another, rather than getting into it, then getting out of it, and then getting back into it again."

Dan Moisand also reads, "everything I can get my hands on." However, he has found at least one learning technique that can beat reading about a topic, and that is writing about it. "I like to write, and it's amazing, when you're putting something together—especially for a client—and you have to write it up, how much more thoroughly you need to be able to grasp the issues you're discussing. The act of writing makes you know all about it."

Just about every publication affecting the financial planning profession comes across my desk, and I've listed some of the key ones, with commentary, in the Resources.

## CONFERENCE TIPS

You could attend some financially oriented conference just about once a week. Even if you had the budget, you certainly don't have the time. However, if you choose the right ones, they can deliver an incredible educational shot in the arm.

"Conferences are the most efficient way of keeping up. At a good conference, you can get the most information in three days," says Ross Levin. Dan Moisand attends "just about every FPA conference" and is planning to attend upcoming NAPFA events. "I like the FPA conferences because of the diversity of attendees. It's very helpful. Also, I attend estate planning conferences at the local estate planning council. They're part of the National Association of Estate Planning Councils. That gives you a different perspective, because it's heavily attorneys."

Of course, if estate planning is not a big part of your practice, you'll probably give that a miss. Your conference list can have a mix of general and specific conferences. Almost every planner should go to the FPA Success Forum, because of the breadth of its sessions and the great networking opportunities. NAPFA organizes a great national conference as well as four regional conferences a year. Although these are geared for the organization's fee-only membership, the high-quality speakers mean that any planners earning a substantial proportion of their income from fees should consider attending. The AICPA has a terrific financial planning conference each year, and even non-CPAs should be able to get a lot out of it.

Like Moisand, you can also attend more specialized conferences. The Investment Management Consultants Association (IMCA) hosts some strong, investment-oriented events. The

Money Management Institute presents seminars on separately managed accounts. If variable annuities make a big part of your practice, you'll want to attend a conference sponsored by the National Association for Variable Annuities.

The big, general conferences tend to get big name speakers, either because they have deep pockets to pay them or because top speakers like being associated with prestigious, well-known conferences. But, if you attend smaller, narrower, more technical conferences, you will find that most—but by no means all—the speakers tend to be, well, less good at speaking. They are invited for their technical skills, which can be formidable, but many have not mastered the rudiments of public speaking.

At one conference that addressed some the legal aspects of estate planning, a very knowledgeable lawyer had written a very knowledgeable article, and she spent an hour reading it aloud. That was it. So, with a few exceptions, the small technical conferences will be high on useful facts, low on startling new insights, and not much value from a networking perspective. But don't discount them on those accounts. If you are heavily involved in estate planning, for example, presentations from CPAs and attorneys who are experts on this field can be invaluable. Sometimes you can run into an Ed Slott, who combines great technical skills with a considerable speaking ability. Just don't expect it all the time.

Nonprofit organizations don't have a monopoly on conferences. Broker-dealers have increasingly elaborate annual events, which can be a combination of sales event and technical seminar. "These broker-dealer conferences get better every year," says John Bowen. Charles Schwab and TD Waterhouse are among the custodians also hosting events for their advisors. The Institute for International Research, a private company despite the academic-sounding name, has a large series of well-organized investing conferences.

Although all these sound exciting, with useful sessions, exciting speakers, and (mostly) glamorous settings, registration fees can be quite steep. When you add hotel and airfare, these events can make a serious dent in your budget, so choose carefully. Fortunately, detailed brochures are usually available well in advance for you to make decisions.

Keep in mind who else will attend—conferences are about a lot more than the sessions. Conferences are about the *hallways*. That's part of what makes FPA Success Forum and the NAPFA annual conference so valuable. It's a chance to hang around at meals, in between sessions, and during evening events to share information and just plain gossip with colleagues. This kind of causal information cannot be picked up from a book or magazine. In fact, I know of one group of high-end advisors who found this hallway time so valuable, they formed their own group just to share information among each other.

At a past NAPFA event, noted financial planning journalist Bob Veres hosted a casual, last minute discussion group after dinner. I attended, figuring I'd be the only one there at an event held so late in what had been a busy day for all the attendees. Well, I was wrong. The conference room was filled to overflowing, and a heated discussion developed and lasted into the night. Again, events like that cannot be duplicated elsewhere.

Conferences also have exhibitors who have the unabashed job to sell. But you can use them to educate yourself. You will find fund managers at many booths. Regarding new software, conferences provide an invaluable chance to see demonstrations of new products. If you are purchasing new products, many companies offer limited-time conference discounts. Even government agencies show up at these—both the IRS and the Social Security Administration have taken booths at conferences to educate planners about their services and policies.

An IRS employee staffing a booth was inviting planners to sign up for informational mailings. One planner refused, saying, "I don't want to give you people any more information about me than I have to." The employee responded, without cracking a smile, "No need to worry, sir. We already know all about you." In fact, government booths have some good information and tables, and both the SSA and IRS produce free electronic newsletters.

## HOW TO READ
## A CONFERENCE SCHEDULE

A young planner who hadn't been to an FPA conference before asked me how one could possibly choose which sessions to attend. Although smaller conferences tend to have only one presentation at a time, the FPA Success Forum and other large conferences have multiple sessions. Even though some may be repeated, it's impossible to hit them all. Look at what fits your practice best, and keep in mind what you may be able to understand largely on your own just by reading notes in the conference binders. In fact, as these huge unwieldy binders give way to easily searchable, data-packed CDs, gleaning the information without attending a session is becoming easier.

However, for very technical details, you'll want to attend in person to hear the explanations and ask questions afterward. The AICPA has always had a technical pensions and benefits conference, well organized and full of details. One year, I found myself sitting at a table asking the attendees—mostly CPAs—why they were at the conference. The most common answer? "Because my firm's managing partner said I had to go." Well, the managing partner was smart. You aren't going to learn material like that anywhere else.

Jeff Kelvin, a lawyer who specializes in investment advisor registration issues, delivers a great conference presentation. He often opens his talk by saying, "I know you don't want to be here. You'd rather be next door, where I understand they're having a seminar on how to get another $10 million under management by the end of the week." But he knows it's important to find out what's new in compliance—and so do the many advisors who fill the room when he speaks. Again, this is material you aren't going to learn elsewhere.

As I'm writing this, I'm trying to figure out which sessions I need to attend for an upcoming 2003 FPA Success Forum. Here's an abbreviated list of the tracks and some of the subjects covered under each.

- *Business solutions.* Benchmarking, technology, outsourcing
- *Estate and tax planning.* Inheritance, family businesses, trust design
- *Investments.* Fixed income, commodities, asset allocation panel with two advisors—Evenksy and Stanasolovich
- *Planning dimensions.* Psychology, managing expectations, goal setting
- *Risk management.* Personal property and liability, life insurance policy management, long-term care
- *Special issues.* Working with expatriates and divorcing clients

Which sessions are useful? They're all useful! Which ones will specifically help your practice? Keeping in mind that you can catch up on some through conference materials, which will you choose? Benchmarking is useful and can be complex. Fortunately, Mark Tibergien is leading this one, and he knows more about this topic than anyone. It may be well worth your time.

Investments? You may be comfortable with what you know. Maybe your practice is limited mostly to mutual funds, annuities, and other, relatively simple products. However, if you've been keeping up with your reading, you may have realized that lawsuits are up: clients are suing planners, charging them with putting them into risky investments and failing to manage risk. Then there's a terrific panel with such leaders as Harold Evensky and Lou Stanasolovich. This is a great opportunity to hear what some leaders are thinking.

The estate and tax planning sessions will be technical and probably merit in-person attention. If you don't do a lot of complex estate planning work, that session may not be necessary. Do you sell or advise on insurance? These risk sessions will be essential. If you don't, again, you may want to skip these.

The key is to think not about what is interesting but what you need. I'm really interested in technology, but by this point, I'm pretty up-to-date on technology as it affects financial planning. However, my knowledge of investing strategies is pretty weak, so I'll probably spend a lot of time in that track.

Ed Slott wrote an article with the kinds of questions you can expect your clients to ask you about IRAs. His hope is that, after reading his article, planners won't get caught looking ignorant on that particular topic. That should be your conference goal: when you get home, you won't look ignorant in front of your clients.

Learning never stops. You've probably figured out already that, in one sense, you never "get there." You're always learning. When I was interviewing planners for this book, even though all of them are successful professionals in mature practices, most of them told me that they were looking forward to seeing what they could learn from the other planners who were quoted. In my experience, the planners who already are considered the best informed have always, and continue, to read the most.

C *a s e* **S** *t u d y*
## LIVE AND LEARN

$C$arl Faulkner and Ken Fielding are partners in a financial planning practice in Los Angeles, and like so many other planners, they are finding themselves squeezed for time. Even with a competent, full-time assistant, they still find themselves trying to do more and more in fewer hours.

"We've been practicing for a while, but I feel more like a beginner every year. Knowledge increases faster than we learn," says Carl. "New laws and regulations, new computer software, new products and services."

"Plus, we're both Certified Financial Planners," says Ken. "So we have our continuing education requirements as well, including a periodic ethics course."

It's been kind of a catch-as-catch-can approach to continuing education and obtaining knowledge generally, but the partners think they can be more effective, and save time, if they become more systematic.

Like most planners, Carl and Ken get a huge number of periodicals: monthly magazines, quarterly newsletters, and weekly bulletins, not to mention the various electronic services that send them specialized publications via e-mail. Most of the publications are free, so they have let them pile up. Some get read; some don't. Some have a lot of useful articles, some have virtually none. The two sit down, and with the help of their assistant, Dennis, they go through every periodical that comes into their office. Ultimately, they find only eight professional publications that really provide practical help. It wasn't necessarily that the others were bad—it's just that they covered information not central to their practice.

"Look at this one," says Carl. "It's all about hedge funds, managed futures, and so on. We don't have any clients in products like these, and I don't think we ever well. Dennis, tell them to stop sending it to us—maybe we can save a few trees."

On the other hand, they find some that they could really use have made their way to the bottom of the pile. They realize that they've been getting a newsletter on REITs but have never really given it a lot of attention, even though they have some clients in real estate. It disappeared under a pile of some larger and glossier, but ultimately less useful, publications.

"I just checked the eight we have left," says Ken, "and found that four give us CE, so they're doubly practical." They divide the publications in half—each partner will be responsible for reading four publications and passing on the useful articles to the other one.

Next on their list are conferences. Even local ones can be expensive, just with admission fees, and when they start figuring in airfare and hotels in other cities, costs really start to add up. Plus, when they're at a conference, they're not minding the practice.

Ken and Carl consider all the conferences coming up, how much they would cost to attend, and how useful each would be. For example, both will attend most of the various meetings of the local state FPA chapters. These are great networking opportunities and, for most events, worth leaving the practice for a day. Both will also attend the FPA Success Forum. There are so many useful sessions, it takes both of them to cover even the most appropriate, let alone all of them.

"One of us definitely has to go to this 529 session. More and more of our clients are asking us about these, and we could use some additional information. But at the same time, there's a session on IRA rollovers. So many of our clients will be facing that in the coming years, any tips and tricks we can pick up will be great," says Carl.

For more specialized conferences, only one will go and bring back notes and any useful conference material. Because Ken is really the investment guy in the partnership, he'll attend an intriguing investment conference in Chicago. The following month, however, Carl will go to a conference on trusts in Dallas—this is his area of expertise. Their custodian also has an annual event, usually somewhere fun, like Orlando or Las Vegas. They will probably alternate who gets to go each year, because it's not as overwhelming as the Success Forum.

A practice management symposium in Sacramento? They'll both give it a miss. "Remember, we went last year," says Carl. "I imagine it was really useful for newbies, but you and I have been in this business for a long time, and there was very little that we didn't know already."

Carl and Ken now feel more in control of information input, but they realize they're just getting started. For example, they can't count on magazines and conferences to keep them entirely up-to-date on regulatory issues. They're a fee-only practice, unaffiliated with a broker-dealer, so they're really on their own when it comes to compliance issues. For years, they've been relying on various consulting services to see them through, and in fact, they have never been cited for any infractions.

However, in the current regulatory atmosphere, they think they had better be a little more proactive. National Regulatory Services has a series of compliance conferences and—even more efficient—Web-based training. "It wouldn't kill us to take a refresher course," says Ken, "plus learn about some of the new regulatory issues."

Ken and Carl also consider the products they've been using. For years, they've relied on a group of mutual funds they've been happy with and a couple of separately managed account providers. But it's been a while since they've taken a good look at what else is out there. "We'll get some ideas from more focused reading," says Carl, "but even these magazines may not be enough. We've kind of closed our doors to a lot of wholesalers. Maybe we should selectively choose some to visit us. Not all of them just come around with nothing but golf balls and glossy brochures. Maybe some of them could really give us a good product demo."

They instruct Dennis to start keeping notes on which companies are calling. Ken and Carl agree to meet for a half hour every week to decide if any of them seem interesting enough to warrant a visit.

"You know," says Dennis, "with the reading and travel you guys are committing to, I have an idea. Most of these magazine articles are available online. If you want, I can download them, burn them into a CD right at my desk, and then you could read them on your laptops while you're on a plane."

"Good idea," says Carl. "It sure beats whatever movie is playing."

"And speaking of movies," says Ken, "I've been hearing more about these Webinars. Various magazines and organizations are having these virtual seminars. They're generally free or low cost. Some are just phone-based, and some have a computer component that allows the speaker to show charts, tables, and full PowerPoint presentations. Some even offer CE credit. Frankly, I didn't want to deal with the technological hassle, but maybe we should reconsider." They agree that Dennis will check the major planning organizations and magazines to see what kinds of virtual seminars they're holding and what they cost.

"We may have a little problem," says Dennis. "For the computer-based chats, I'm not sure our computers can handle the necessary software. We're using three-year-old machines, and I'm not even sure if what we have is the latest. I don't know enough about computers to know if we even need an upgrade. Maybe we could use some technology lessons as well. I'm wondering if we'd be more efficient with more modern machines. I know you had a speaker at the last state FPA meeting who was a technology consultant. Maybe he could tell us what we're missing—we could see if we have any IT gaps."

The partners agree. "He spoke about using technology more efficiently, but I didn't see a problem with our firm, so I didn't really think he was talking to us. Maybe there's more we could be doing. Call him up," says Ken. "See what he can do for us and what he charges."

Three months later, although Ken and Carl are busy as ever, they feel they have more control over their practice. They have planned their conference attendance over the next eight months and mapped out the key sessions they need to attend. Although a number of wholesalers and other salespeople have wasted their time, several truly educated them, and in one case, they actually latched onto a new product that would help several of their clients.

They tried to participate in their first Webinar, but the computer kept crashing on them, and Carl and Ken swore they would never try another one. But that was before the tech consultant came—and told them their computers were laughably out of date. A few weeks and a new system later, a Webinar went smoothly, helping them update themselves on SMAs and throwing an hour of CE credit into the bargain.

Carl screens every new publication that comes into the office, and the partners decide if it's worth adding to the official reading list or not and, if so, which partner would be the most appropriate one to read it.

At the FPA Success Forum the following year, Carl tells Ken that he remembers what a favorite philosophy professor said on the first day of class: "I am a teacher of philosophy and a student of philosophy. I could not be a teacher if I weren't also a student." Reflects Carl, "I guess that's true of financial planners, too."

# EXECUTIVE SUMMARY

- Every planner needs to find an efficient way to keep up with new compliance, product, and practice issues.
- Compliance is not a do-it-yourself project. You can and should rely on your broker-dealer and consulting firm. However, you still have to keep up yourself.
- An RIA consulting firm can review your ADV, perform mock audits, and review your advertising, among other services.
- Beyond advertising, you have to keep up with other issues, such as how new tax laws will affect client portfolios and whether you should use certain new products.
- Conferences, periodicals, study groups, and even salespeople are good sources of information.
- In a larger firm, different staff members can be responsible for different areas, and information can be shared.

- Conferences are expensive but extremely useful. Consider both general conferences and narrow, technical ones that fit your practice.
- At bigger conferences, choose sessions carefully to fill gaps in your knowledge.
- At any conference, make sure to spend a lot of time in the "hallway," talking with your colleagues and other professionals.
- Be sure to visit exhibitors as well—they can be educational, especially if you can schedule technology demos.

# 9

# BUILDING AN EMPIRE— AND SELLING IT

**W**hen I was growing up, there was a family-owned children's clothing store down the block from our apartment house. The founding generation was long gone, the second generation was ready to retire, and the third generation was uninterested. The family sold the store to some would-be entrepreneurs who decided to "fix" the store. Unfortunately, they didn't realize that what they were buying was not really the stock but the relationships with local customers who had been shopping there for years. These customers didn't want to see changes in a store on which they had relied for years. The new owners destroyed the relationships—and the store disappeared.

It's the same thing with the buying and selling of a practice. Such a deal can take care of two big issues: for the buyer, it's a way to grow quickly; for the seller, the sale provides a graceful and, if done properly, well-funded exit. But both have to be aware that what is really being purchased is relationships. Both the seller, and especially the buyer, have to consider whether the clients being transferred will fit with the model and personality of the new planner.

When two practices merge, it's pretty much the same situation. Although the old clients will still, presumably, deal with the same planner they've always had, different cultures in the two firms will create problems. The synergies, the scales of economy, that led two or more practitioners to throw in their lots with each other will disappear, if that's the case. With financial planning practices, it's all about the relationships, and nowhere does this become more obvious than when practices are purchased or merged.

There are also financial complexities in the process. Not only do the two parties have to figure out how much a practice is worth but how and when will the price be paid and how much overlap the retiring planner will have with the purchaser.

But, if the psychological factors and financial terms can be worked out, the buying/selling or merging of a practice can benefit all parties involved, including the clients. These transactions are still new in the financial planning profession but are becoming more common. "It's a great time to buy or sell," says John Bowen, who thinks more brokers will be getting into the act to facilitate the purchases.

I've added some interesting survey results about the buying and selling of practices throughout this chapter. Figures 9.1 and 9.2 show key trends in the selling of practices.

## YES, NO, OR MAYBE

Some planners I spoke with have been through, or are intending to go through, merger or purchase; others would consider it under the right circumstances; and a third group has ruled it out entirely.

**FIGURE 9.1**  *Median Selling Prices*

The median selling prices for advisory practices continued to rise, even while the stock market was plunging. (Source: FP Transitions)

**FIGURE 9.2**  *The Ratio of Selling Prices to Annual Practice Revenues*

This backs up the previous figure on median prices. As FP Transitions notes, "It seems that the revenue streams of advisory practices are at least as valuable today as ever." (Source: FP Transitions)

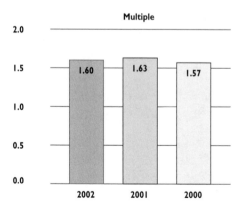

Nancy Langdon Jones has viewed the process from both angles. Earlier in her career, she bought a practice and is now considering selling her own in preparation for retirement.

When she bought a practice, "The other planner and I did it ourselves and signed over all the clients in three months." The terms were a three-year buyout with payments coming from quarterly cash flow. "This ensured that we'd both participate in market fluctuations." It also placed the seller's best interest in keeping in close touch with Jones, because her ultimate price depended on client retention. "We were both very happy with the result." In fact, she has a similar arrangement with the colleague who will begin purchasing her practice, starting this year.

It's great when the situation works out like that. "Selling to a younger staff member is a great way to transition," says Deena Katz. However, you have be very careful. She continues, "There's an awful lot to know about, and I would use a professional to help with the purchase." Many would-be mergers or buyouts don't happen because the cultures are so different.

Like Jones, Amy Leavitt is also selling her practice to an employee, in an arrangement that takes into account both their clients' feelings and the employee's history with the firm. "He's been intimately involved with clients on a long-term basis, and little by little over the years, he's been doing more and more." To prepare the clients, she sent them a letter saying that he is becoming more and more an owner. She also explained that her role within the firm would continue to evolve toward more portfolio design. "We let the clients know that nothing has really changed, but we want to let them know what is happening."

Leavitt and her employee have a revenue-sharing arrangement. They're splitting the profits on a formula, where each year Leavitt take less and he takes more. "It's not totally arm's length—he helped me build this, and he didn't get paid for what he was putting in during the lean years. So, in a sense, I'm giving him the business in part, even though there's an earn-out." So Leavitt didn't feel the need to go through an elaborate appraisal process. "We agreed that this proposal made sense."

Group practices are becoming more prevalent, she believes, and such practices will create natural successors within that. The succession plan is just another piece of the model for running your practice. "When we coach financial planners, we look at it as a pyramid. At the bottom are your values and vision—what do you want the practice to look like? Then you go up and have a marketing plan and a strategic business plan. Then you go further up: what is your cycle, and how do you deliver plans? Then up to practice management, and then practice transition. It's a hierarchy—the issues you face." She advises planners to set up a practice as a business early, for succession purposes, so that they have flexibility down the road.

Jeff Rattiner acquired a tax practice with about 130 clients last year. But he has some reservations about sole proprietorships. "Buying a small firm like that is tough. The person who runs it *is* the business. If that person is not involved, what are you buying?"

Katz echoes Rattiner: "At any rate, you need to have some kind of business succession plan, if you have a *business*. If you have a *practice*, you don't care. Your clients may care, and this may be a disservice to them, but you need some way to have your business outlasting you." Practice or business? That's the difference. "When it's just you and your practice, it all depends on you and your personality. The more you can systematize and spread out the responsibility, the more attractive you are for sale." If all you have to sell are client relationships, believes Katz, succession will be a lot more difficult.

Other planners have even more reservations. All of Ric Edelman's growth has been from within, not from purchases. "It is something I'd consider, but we have not attempted to do it as yet. We've toyed with it, I know how to do it, and I know what I would do with it if I did that."

Sheryl Garrett pretty much rules it out altogether. "We've absolutely never considered buying another practice. Most of our clients have never been to another planner. Establishing expectations on how we work and how relationships will work is much easier when they *don't* have preconceived notions." She finds that, when a new client comes to her practice having already worked with another advisor, the engagement often becomes challenging. "The former advisor trained them in their way, and my model is different. They have to unlearn a lot of things. I think it would be a nightmare to buy another practice. Someone would have to *pay* me to take over someone else's practice. So much more work than clients from scratch."

She admits that her situation is unusual—and in fact, her network model allows for rapid growth without purchases. "But the only way I'd buy is if practice was just like mine."

Not rushing into anything either is Ross Levin, although he does want to continue to grow. "Our ultimate objective is to have the practice last longer than we do." He said he'd consider some kind of consortium—more of a sharing arrangement than a merger. "It's hard to merge. We've got very personal relationships with clients, whom we've kind of handpicked, and we're really careful about who we take on as clients. They screen us and we screen them. It could happen, but we're not really considering that right now."

However, he says he might add principals who can bring clients with them. "One of our principals, Kathy Longo, came from a family office, and so she had some clients and a similar way of doing things, so it was seamless bringing her in. But that can be a hard thing to do."

Lou Stanasolovich has similar reservations. "I've looked at the idea of buying a practice, and I'm not sure that makes sense. Most practices out there don't deliver the kinds of clients we're looking for today." He also has business reservations. "People want a lot of money for their practice, and it's hard to justify for us. Say you pay twice annual revenues for a practice, so we spend $2 million for a $1 million practice. We spread that cost over five years, which equals $400,000 a year. But we're only taking in $1 million, and that's without financing costs. You're presuming a 70 percent margin there, and can you really get that? At one times revenues it might work, but not twice. At least, not for us."

## A RECIPE FOR SUCCESS

Dan Moisand engineered a successful merger of his one-professional practice with a larger firm, but only after a lot of thought and painstaking research. Although he eventually merged his practice successfully, before he reached a good conclusion, he wrote up his ongoing experiences in what became an award-winning article for the *Journal of Financial Planning:* "The Urge to Merge: Insights from a Sole Practitioner's Search for Partners." Although Moisand was doing fine on his own, he liked being part of a team, so he set about to become part of one. In the article, he wrote, "I learned that high-level, conceptual issues need to be tackled early and quickly with experienced practitioners."

One planner looked promising, and they complemented each other nicely. Moisand was younger and felt he had failed to land certain clients because they thought he was too young. The other practitioner felt he had lost out because some thought him too old. In other places, too, they matched nicely, but some areas turned out to be too difficult to overcome. The other planner billed hourly, for example, and that didn't suit Moisand's practice. So, although Moisand continues to have a lot of respect for him, he realized a merger would not work.

The difficulties led Moisand to draw up a list of things to watch out for when going through the merger process. Here are some of them.

- *Regulatory issues.* If you are thinking about merging with a firm affiliated with a different broker-dealer, or a different custodial firm, the necessary changes may not be impossible, but they will be very difficult.

- *Philosophies.* Make sure that you have the same thoughts about what kinds of funds to use, how big the merged firm should grow, and how the compensation structure should work, for example.
- *Focus.* Throughout the process, think about your clients. Don't neglect them while you look, and consider how they will be served in a proposed merger.
- *Problems.* Don't expect a merger to make life perfectly smooth. The merger may take care of some issues but introduce others, like giving you more people to manage and making you share decision-making responsibilities.

Moisand's August 2002 article is available online at the *Journal of Financial Planning* Web site <www.fpanet.org/journal/>. It is essential reading for any planner considering a merger.

## LOOKING AT THE DOLLARS AND CENTS

Increasingly, for those who want help selling their practice, there is help. Broker-dealers increasingly are getting into the act, helping retiring planners to sell their practices to planners who will continue the relationship with the clients and the broker-dealer. Speaking of her broker-dealer, Leavitt said, "Lincoln has an excellent plan for transition, and I leveraged off some of the resources from that program," when arranging for her sale.

Probably no third party has given more thought to the issues surrounding buying and selling practices than David Grau, president of Business Transitions, which runs FP Transitions, a Web site—indeed a system—for buying and selling practices. No planner should try to buy or sell a practice without having a look at the FP Transitions site and considering them as a broker for the transition. Grau has probably seen more deals and

almost-deals than he can count, and he has drawn some conclusions about what works and doesn't and how you should approach the process.

"The one thing all sellers are interested in is their value.
'What am I worth?' Surprisingly enough, when we opened our
site, we thought everyone would want to go out and obtain a
formal valuation and have a written 80-page opinion justifying
their price, so they could say, 'See, I am worth this.'"

But he was wrong. "We found that maybe 1 or 2 out of every
100 would pay the money and take the time to have a formal
valuation done." But they did find that the buy-sell model ultimately depended on a "multiple basis" or rule of thumb. For
example, he said, medical, dental, and veterinary practices
tended to sell for a multiple about 65 to 85 percent of annual
gross revenue. CPAs tend to sell for about 1 to 1.25 times annual gross revenue, and everyone thought that would be the
financial planning range. "But advisors are already up to *twice*
gross revenue (recurring revenue), and some think that is still
low. They've only been selling these practices in an organized
fashion for four or five years, and already they're twice as valuable as a CPA practice."

A financial planning practice has special advantages and
problems. "You are buying future income streams, with relatively low overhead." Yes, a doctor's patients return for check-
ups every year, and an accountant's clients come back for tax
preparation every year. "But with recurring income, you have a
predictable stream attached. And that doubles the value. When
we see people get a formal valuation, it comes out to what a
CPA firm would be valued. And for a buyer, that's good. But the
market will pay about twice that."

For this kind of figure, however, Grau had to make certain
assumptions—which you also have to make if you are in a buying
or selling position. "We assume the seller will help deliver those
clients, with no additional costs for doing this. This should lead
to a 90 percent transfer rate at minimum, and we almost always

achieve this goal. We assume the practice is in a metropolitan area, because it improves demand for the practice. We assume the down payment will be about 30 percent of the purchase price. Last year's average was 28 percent. We assume the sale will be of assets, not stock. And finally, we assume the balance is paid over three to five years, using seller financing." Figure 9.3 shows that the average down payment has edged up, while Figure 9.4 shows that financing terms have gone down recently.

That's the kicker. This process is still new, and according to Grau, banks are still reluctant to finance these transitions. "So seller financing is key."

**FIGURE 9.3** *Average Down Payment*

Average down payment is up. FP Transitions says this reflects both increased demand for practices and a strengthening market. The company reports: "Virtually all the practices sold on our system these days are sold on an earn-out basis, where the buyer pays some amount of cash up front and the seller finances the remaining balance over some time, usually between three and four years. So the increase in the average down payment signals the stiff competition to buy a practice today, as well as a willingness on the part of today's buyers to shoulder a growing portion of the risk involved in transferring a seller's clients to the new owner." (Source: FP Transitions)

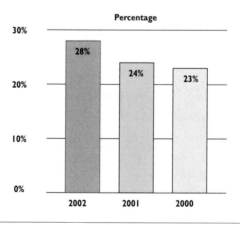

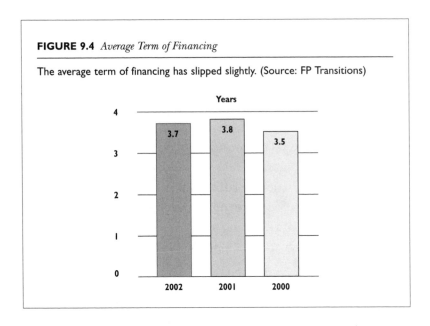

**FIGURE 9.4** *Average Term of Financing*

The average term of financing has slipped slightly. (Source: FP Transitions)

In this model, Grau expects the seller will accept 70 percent of the purchase price in the form of capital gains tax treatment and about 30 percent as ordinary treatment. The IRS will make its judgment based on the transaction. "They look for a written agreement and an arm's length transaction. And they tend to respect the decisions of the parties as long as they're reasonable and based on a solid tax foundation."

You can't look at a purchase as just one item, especially for tax purposes. "When you buy and sell a practice, it's many components, and that's why it's an asset purchase. The assets that get bought and sold, even in a simple practice, are the seller's goodwill, client list, physical client files, and the seller's assistance in delivering those files." There might be some file cabinets, computers, and software. "And of course, there is always the seller's agreement not to compete and not to solicit that client base. And while those are bundled up and called *the practice* and given a single value, the IRS unbundles them and gives each one a separate tax treatment."

For example, continues Grau, when you buy seller's goodwill and client list and files, that is slated for capital gains treatment for the seller and a 15-year depreciation rate for the buyer. Continued assistance, however, is labor: ordinary income to the seller, and an immediate deductible expense to the buyer as it is paid. It's like hiring an independent contractor. File cabinets have different write-off periods from electronic equipment. The noncompete/nonsolicit agreement is ordinary income to the seller and a 15-year depreciation to the buyer. "It's important when you buy a practice that you understand this—what you're buying and how you're paying for it."

There are some special aspects of small shops, says Grau, that buyers should be aware of. "A lot of the time, sellers, because they're one-principal shops, have some leeway, and they take advantage of it. They run every possible deduction through their books. Things such as gifts, travel, a lease on the Lexus." Because these are asset purchases on a buyer's part, and it's a one-principal shop buying a one-principal shop, the buyers typically don't buy the liabilities and expenses. So the fact that someone let the expenses go up may make no difference to a buyer.

Buyers should see what has driven up expenses, says Grau. They may be up because there is an inefficient system or because everyone gets a free, 80-page plan every 6 months or face-to-face quarterly meetings. Those things are hard to fix. "But if expenses are up just because they ran things through the business, most buyers just buy the client list and income streams and take it back to their own roofs."

High-overhead and low-overhead one-principal firms, says Grau, will sell for the same amount (or at least the same multiple of gross revenue). When people get formal valuations from various accounting firms, they will say, "Well, you have 60 percent overhead. But it's not always a problem, because it's not being bought."

# CONSIDERING THE INTANGIBLES

But Grau, like Moisand, agrees that there is a lot more to buying and selling than how the ledgers work out. Consider the conventional wisdom that sole practitioners cannot sell their practices, because there is nothing to sell except the personality of the owner.

"This isn't a problem," said Grau. "Our typical buyer and seller are one-principal firms—that is, firms with one shareholder. That's probably 99 percent of our clientele. Some of them have a $700,000–$800,000 income range with one principal and five to six employees."

The problem with selling these could have stemmed from the lack of transfer structure in the profession, says Grau, not an inherent lack of value in a small practice. Consider a typical, 20-year-old, fee-only practice with 50 clients and $35 million in assets under management. This could generate $350,000 to $400,000 a year. "In the past you'd ask a friend or two or run an anonymous ad in a local paper. But anytime you have a seller going to a buyer asking if they'll take it off your hands, the value just goes down." But FP Transitions, says Grau, can work to find a local buyer who has a good match with the personality and business philosophy of the seller.

Grau doesn't make the mistake of discounting philosophy. Successful planners put their clients first when considering selling. Grau expected that when the markets began to go up after the Iraq war wound down, planners would see a chance to sell their practices on the upswing. But it seems that many didn't want to look as though they were bailing out on their clients. "Most sellers don't make top dollar the number one priority, because they know they're going to see former clients on the golf course, at social clubs, and downtown. So they pick someone who can step into their shoes after they leave and keep it running almost just like it was. For example, fee-only sellers, every time, will sell to a fee-only buyer. And a local purchaser is preferred 85 percent of the time. Same gender is also preferred. Women would rather sell to a woman. And those affiliated with a broker-dealer want the buyer to keep the same affiliation."

In fact, sellers often put restrictions on the buyer during the finance period, barring them from changing phone numbers, addresses, broker-dealers, buildings, or schedules. Grau says, "They want to keep it as similar as possible."

## DOING THE PREP WORK

When you go to buy a house, you expect to see that the owners have spruced up the place—perhaps put on a coat of paint, repaired the cracks in the driveway, or trimmed the hedges. But oddly, the reverse seems to be true among sellers of practices, and Grau doesn't see that as a good idea.

"When we see a practice come up for sale, this is what has typically happened. They have been thinking about selling for two to three years, and they have been spending more time away from the business, bringing in fewer clients, hiring employees to cover the owner's absence. "So, as a percentage, the expenses jump up. And quality and attention to clients goes down." Revenues level off or decline.

But although this is a bad idea for the seller, it's a good trend for the buyer. "They're thinking the opposite. They say to themselves, 'Hey, if I buy these assets now, I spend less money. In a few years I can restore the income stream." They have a line of credit for the down payment, or they borrow from their family. They scoop up the clients without the trouble and expense of marketing. "The rest of the purchase price is taken out of cash flow, and eventually you own 100 percent of the equity."

The sellers are hurting themselves and, again, helping the buyers, by acting rashly. Says Grau, "Many sellers come to us almost impulsively. I don't think there's a whole lot of advanced thought to it. For every one we talk to a year or two in advance, there's ten we never heard of before that list for an immediate sale."

## INTO THE FUTURE

Practice reorganization—the buying and selling of practices—is growing in importance, but there's still a bit of the Wild West about it. Accounting practices have probably been actively bought and sold for a century. In fact, a division of Business Transitions has recently started brokering the buying and selling of accounting practices, and Grau says it will likely surpass the financial planning division soon in terms of numbers of practices. It's a stable multiple, he says, that everyone understands. "There's a long history of buying and selling."

But if you're just starting out now, then by the time you're ready to bow out, the situation may have changed. "We're hopeful that if we can plug in some kind of bank financing, like a GMAC turnkey financing that doesn't take six months like an Small Business Administration loan, that values will go up because demand will go up. For now, banks want to see hard collateral, and a lot of practices are file cabinets and a computer system. There is nothing else." The same could be said about accounting practices, but, "They've done them before, and there's a track record—nothing fancy, but predictable."

Already, Grau is seeing more bank loans, at least for the larger, more mature practices. (So Deena Katz and others may be right that it's tougher to sell a small firm.) But in five to six years, says Grau, those loans will be paid off, and banks may feel more optimistic.

Also driving the trend may be a tendency toward greater profitability in larger firms. See Figure 9.5.

Perhaps someday, thinks Grau, he'll be able to show banks a list of 45 practices that were purchased on loan with no defaults

**FIGURE 9.5** *Revenue per Client*

Here's an argument for merging and growing larger: Bigger firms simply garner more money from each client. A bigger firm may be able to run more efficiently, with more support staff, for example. But this doesn't mean smaller practices are unprofitable or a mistake. It's about how you want to practice. (Source: Moss Adams)

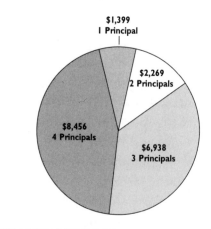

$1,399
1 Principal

$2,269
2 Principals

$8,456
4 Principals

$6,938
3 Principals

and no collateral. At that time, banks may recognize the list of clients—the relationships themselves—as collateral. "Then, more sales at better value should result."

C *a s e* S *t u d y*
## PEAS IN A POD

Life has been good to Al Wharton. He has built a solid practice in a densely packed suburban town. He is the sole owner of his firm, and he has two additional CFPs and several support staff. His mixed fee and commission practice has been so successful, in fact, that he has been honored by Acme Financial, his broker-dealer.

But Al thinks he can be bigger, and he would like to get bigger faster, not just by adding clients here and there over the months and years. He'd like to add another practice entirely and knows that he can merge with another practice of a similar size, taking on another partner in the process, or even buy another practice outright.

In fact, he's already been approached by another firm, a three-partner firm in the city, whose founding partner has been a friend of Al's since the two found themselves on the same state FPA committee several years ago. "It would be great for all of us," says Harry. "You'd become our fourth partner. You'd keep your office—it would essentially be our suburban outpost. Many of our clients live in your area but work near ours, so we could reach them in either area. We're both reps at Acme, so we wouldn't have to do any switching. We'd both save money— our office manager already told us she's retiring at the end of the year. We wouldn't replace her—your office manager would become the firm's manager, because we don't need two."

That makes a lot of sense. Al has a pretty good idea of how well Harry's firm is doing, and vice versa, and they would be a good match. Al turns to the young woman at the desk next to his. "So, should I merge? I'd spend less time doing a lot of the grunt work, more time planning. More money, too, because of the scale efficiencies."

"I'm just a college freshman, Dad," she says. "But I know you'd hate having to get the approval of other partners before making a decision. You always like having it your own way. Maybe you could handle having one partner, but three? You know and like Harry, but you scarcely know his partners. I think you'd be miserable."

Harry knows his daughter is right.

He calls the marketing director at Acme. "Jane? Al Wharton here. How are you doing? Listen, I remember at the annual rep meeting several months ago, you said Acme was in the process of creating a list of practices that were looking to merge or sell out. I wonder if you've gotten anywhere yet."

"Not formally, but there have been inquiries. Let me go over my notes and get back to you in a few days. I'll let you know if anyone in your area has expressed an interest in selling or merging."

Jane calls back at the end of the week. "There's something that may interest you. Now, you live in Millerton. There's a sole practitioner about 40 miles further out, if I'm reading this map right, in a town called Carlton Creek. Know of it?"

"Sure. It's really too far out for a commute into the city, not near any commuter lines, but there's a big pharmaceutical company out there."

"He probably gets a lot of his clients from them, I guess. At any rate, his name is Sanford Doyle, and I'll give you his number. He told us he's thinking of retiring and would like to transition out of his practice. If that's not too far, it just might work out. If the two of you proceed with this, keep us in the loop. We'll help any way we can."

Al calls Sanford the next day and introduces himself. Sanford invites Al to come up to his office and learn more about his practice. He explains that he rents a one-room office in an executive suite. "This town actually supports a fair number of professionals. In addition to the pharmaceutical firm—where I get most of my clients—there's an agricultural college, so there's a prosperous professional clientele here."

When Al gets to town, Sanford shows him around, then sketches some generalities about his firm's financial status. "I'll be honest. I haven't done any heavy marketing in the last couple of years. That's meant fewer clients, as some of my older ones died. Also, some retired down South and wanted to work with someone local. But I still have a good list of loyal clients, for whom I do comprehensive planning and sell mutual funds. I have a few high-end clients who are in separately managed accounts, and I sell a lot of annuities as well. I've had a practice here for 30 years, so I'm well known."

"It sounds like you've earned a lot of loyalty here," says Al. "Are you staying in town when you retire? Would you be willing to work closely with me to transition your clients, to make them comfortable with new faces? Also, I'd like you to help me with connections to the college and the pharmaceutical firm."

"Help you? I'd insist on it," laughs Sanford. "My wife and I have no plans to live anywhere else. My CLU is so old it's written on parchment, and I believe I was the first Certified Financial Planner in the tricounty area. I have a commitment to these people. If my clients feel I've just dumped them to retire, I couldn't hold my head up around here."

Despite the differences between Millerton and Carlton Creek, Al's and Sanford's client rosters are surprisingly similar—heavily professional, mostly families. Al thinks he'd be comfortable taking on the list.

"Would you continue to maintain an office here?" asks Sanford. "People think very locally here. I think they'd be unhappy about traveling to your office. This office is actually within walking distance of many of my clients."

"I agree," says Al. "I'm plenty busy in my office, but I have two CFPs working for me. One is considerably more senior, and giving him control of what would become my second office would be a good experience for him. And he already lives north of our office, so this wouldn't be adding much to his commute."

The two men are silent for a few moments. "I think," said Al, "we need to talk numbers."

In the coming weeks, Al and Sanford hammer out a deal. Sanford is happy to get a comfortable fee that will heavily augment his retirement. Al feels he's getting a great deal—he's comfortable he can build the business back to its peak, and even beyond, with some aggressive marketing. As he thought, the more senior of his two planners is delighted with the new assignment, and Sanford makes plans to hire a junior planner to replace him in the home office.

Al and Sanford visit various banks, where they are known, to arrange financing. The banks are sympathetic—but that's it. The planners are disappointed but not surprised. "It's clear that we have two solid businesses here," says one loan officer. "But this is still new—we don't have a handle on financial planning practices, and a deal like this would never get by the bank's senior VP. There's no long history of selling practices like yours, and banks like ours don't have a sense of our risk." He shows them to the door and hits an optimistic note. "But, when you're ready to retire, Al, I'm sure things will have changed."

"I'll keep that in mind," says Al dryly.

They fall back onto plan B. "I'll dip into my capital and pay you 30 percent up front," says Al. Sanford will finance the rest over three years—and agrees to work on delivering his clients over the same period. They further agree that after the deal closes, Al's associate will start going to Carlton Creek, and Al will introduce all of his clients in a series of face-to-face meetings over the coming months. Al will get up to Carlton Creek himself at least one day a month. They will work together on a memo to all the clients explaining the transfer—stressing that this will be a comfortable, gradual process that continues to leave all client accounts at Acme. The broker-dealer is pleased that all the money stays in the family and sets about helping Al and Sanford with the necessary paperwork.

"One more thing," says Sanford. "I always rented a room at the local hotel every December and held a holiday party for all my clients. Because so many of them know each other and know me personally, it's almost a family gathering. Will you continue this?"

"We have a similar event at our firm, but I don't want anyone overwhelmed by a lot of new faces in a new location. This year, and probably next, we'll have a Millerton event for my old clients, and Carlton Creek event for yours, but my entire staff will attend—and you too, of course—to help everyone get used to the new management."

Over her next college vacation, months after all the papers have been signed, Al's daughter is back in the office, helping out to make a few extra dollars for the next semester. "How's it working with the new practice?" she asks.

"It's slow. But we've kept virtually every one of the old clients and have already signed a number of new ones. So the firm is actually a little bigger than when we bought it. Of course, it's been a big hassle merging their record system with ours . . ."

"It would've been a lot easier just to merge with Harry's firm, wouldn't it?"

"Probably." He sighs.

"But you're happier this way, aren't you?"

"Yes," he says. "Yes, I am.

---

## EXECUTIVE SUMMARY

- It is possible to grow your practice by merging or buying another one, and selling can be a graceful and profitable way to retire.
- Any change in ownership must take into account personalities and practice philosophies.
- If you sell to an employee, the buyer already knows the practice philosophy, and your clients are guaranteed some continuity.
- Small practices are sometimes at a disadvantage, because their value is tightly bound to the owner.
- Mergers only work when the financial, psychological, and practice situations all mesh; any disconnects are a recipe for disaster.

- Selling a practice can be a complex financial issue as well, with the IRS treating various aspects of the practice differently.
- Sellers can put themselves at a disadvantage, and give buyers an edge, by letting their practices slip during the final years.
- Seller financing is common, because outside financing is hard to get, and it helps ensure that the seller cooperates during the transition period.
- FP Transitions is pioneering the use of third-party brokers to facilitate sales.

For some chapters, I've identified places to get more information to help you apply the advice in the chapters.

# CHAPTER I

## Executive Suites

Many companies either provide and manage executive suites or organize listings of companies that do operate regionally. Unless you're in a very rural area (and there are even executive suites in Alaska), there's a good chance of finding some options near you. The companies below all operate nationally but not necessarily in every state. The services available, terms, and costs can vary widely, but these Web sites can give you a good idea of what you're going to get before even picking up a phone.

- *Esuite.com <www.esuite.com>.* A free service for searching for executive suites in your area. Search by city, metro area, state, or Zip code. You can even request locations that have specialized services, such as a high-speed Internet connection.
- *HQ Global Workplaces <www.hq.com>.* Search for locations in about 30 states. HQ provides a wide range of services and has packages especially designed for the independent professional.
- *Alliance Business Centers <www.abcn.com>.* They have offices in most states, and their Web site allows you to take a virtual tour through a sample Alliance office.

- *Officescape <www.officescape.com>*. Access instant prices and service descriptions in scores of locations.
- *Abacus Serviced Offices <www.serviced-offices.biz>*. Their listings give price ranges, a description of services, exterior photos, and—especially helpful—information on access by car and public transportation.

# CHAPTER 2

## Technology Research

This list is by no means comprehensive. Rather, you should look at this as a minimum. Even if you outsource your technology needs completely, you still have to know what's available.

- The New York Times, *Circuits section, every Thursday <www .nytimes.com>*. A lot of coverage here is on games and similar topics, but the Q&A section will likely answer some of your most perplexing questions. The reviews of major new software initiatives are extremely helpful. Sign up for journalist David Pogue's free, weekly newsletter.
- The Wall Street Journal, *technology section, every Thursday. <www.wsj.com>*. Few journalists cover technology as clearly as Walt Mossberg.
- Inc. *magazine <www.inc.com>*. *Inc.* offers a free, small-business technology newsletter.
- *What Is <www.whatis.com>*. This is a magnificent cheat sheet. Pretty much any technical term or file format you come across, but don't understand, is described here in non-technical language.
- The Journal of Accountancy *<www.aicpa.org>*. This magazine from the AICPA has a monthly technology Q&A, centering mostly on Excel and Word. Editor Stanley Zaro-

win, who has been covering these issues since before Windows, answers questions in great detail.

- *Trade magazines.* All the major magazines cover industry-specific software.
  - Financial Planning *<www.financial-planning.com>*. John Olsen, one of the planners interviewed in this text, moderates an online discussion board on software. Partners at Etelligent Consulting, also quoted in this book, frequently post here as well.
  - The Journal of Financial Planning *<www.fpanet.org>*.
  - Investment News *<www.investmentnews.com>*.
  - Bloomberg Wealth Manager *<wealth.bloomberg.com/>*.
  - Investment Advisor *<www.ia-mag.com>*. Andy Gluck, who commented in the Web section, is a regular contributor.
  - Financial Advisor *<www.financialadvisormagazine.com>*.
- *Books.* As I noted, most technology books are poorly focused for a planner's needs and get out-of-date too quickly. But make an exception for the exceptional *Virtual Office Tools for a High Margin Practice: How Client-Centered Financial Advisors Can Cut Paperwork, Overhead, and Wasted Hours,* by David J. Drucker and Joel P. Bruckenstein.
- *Conferences.* The technology tracks at any of the major financial planning conferences will be well worth your time. Also, nothing can replace a few minutes spent at a conference booth.

## Software for Financial Planners

Again, this is not a comprehensive list but a good place to start.

- *Annual software survey,* Financial Planning Magazine *<www.financial-planning.com>*. This lists the major financial planning features and products. It is the most comprehensive listing available of financial planning software.

- *Etelligent Consulting* <*www.etelligentconsulting.com*>. Their Web site links to professional planning software companies in six categories: portfolio management, client relationship management, financial planning, asset allocation, document imaging, and research.
- *The Gregory Group* <*www.gregory-group.com*>. The Gregory Group offers free resources on their Web site, and founder Kip Gregory is one of the top speakers and consultants on technology and financial planning.
- *Back-up systems.*
  - *Iron Mountain* <*www.ironmountain.com*>. Originally a traditional, off-site paper documents storage company, it has branched out into electronic storage. It advertises compliance with various regulators.
  - *Xdrive* <*www.xdrive.com*>. It can simply back up all of your key PC files in a single account.
  - *Iomega* <*www.iomega.com*>. This company created the common Zip and Jaz drives, which use disks that can be rerecorded again and again.
  - I wrote an article about backing up in the November 2001 issue of *Financial Planning*. Some of the prices may be out-of-date, but the concepts and companies are still around. Read the article at <www.financial-planning.com/pubs/fp/20011101021.html>.
- *PDA software.* These products are useful for handheld computers running the Palm operating system.
  - *Documents to Go* <*www.dataviz.com*>. This suite of products lets you view and, often, edit such formats as Word, Excel, graphics, PDF, PowerPoint, and e-mail. I've found it absolutely essential. Add a portable keyboard, and you have a superlight laptop that can do much of what a computer costing ten times as much can do.

- *Agendus <www.imabic.com>.* This program supercharges both your handheld organization and the desktop system with a corresponding Windows product. It offers more options than the standard Palm system for To Do, Memos, and other applications.
- *Palmsource <www.palmsource.com>.* Probably the most complete and best-organized collection of software for the Palm-based heldheld. A word of advice: the usefulness and quality of programs offered vary widely. Most companies give you a trial run before you actually buy anything, and I suggest you do that. Do this when you have some spare time—installing and learning a new program takes some time.
- *Web design help.*
  - *Advisorsquare <www.advisorsquare.com>.* This company reaches out to financial professionals in particular. This company promises that its AdvisorMail system "meets all SEC/NASD/NYSE regulatory guidelines for broker-dealer e-mail monitoring and storage."
  - *AdvisorProducts <www.advisorproducts.com>.* President and CEO Andy Gluck, who was quoted extensively in the Web section, has become synonymous with Web site design and management for financial planners.
- *Contact management.* Your choices will depend on whether you have 200 clients or 2,000 and whether a broker-dealer or custodial system coordinates with your desktop. The following software products are some of the most highly regarded. Contact management can be a very personal decision, so don't buy a system until you have given it a thorough test drive. Switching later on can be a major hassle.
  - *Goldmine <www.goldmine.com>.* With various suites, you can get more ways of organizing dates and more bells and whistles than you can imagine.
  - *Act! <www.act.com>.* Another well-known program with an amazing array of features.

- *Microsoft Outlook* <www.microsoft.com>. This can be cumbersome, in my opinion, but it probably came with your computer anyway. To be fair, the way it integrates e-mail and other information has made it a favorite product with a lot of small businesses.
- *A Palm System* (see above). Make your Palm contact program your contact manager. It's not as fancy as Goldmine or Act!, but it easily backs onto your PDA. You also may be able to coordinate your PDA with Goldmine or ACT!
- *Miscellaneous.*
  - *Adobe Acrobat* <www.adobe.com>. It's not so much the price—about $500—that can be daunting but the learning curve. Still, once you get up-to-speed, this program is terrific at helping you prepare beautiful plans with well-integrated charts and tables. You may not have to buy it; in fact, it is often incorporated into top financial planning products. It's worth taking the time to learn.
  - *Dragon Naturally Speaking* <www.naturalspeak.com>. This is probably the best-known speech recognition software. It requires some patience to set it up the first time— the software has to "learn" your voice patterns. But, once it gets going, it is remarkably accurate.
  - *Efax* <www.efax>. I've always hated fax machines—I hate standing there, watching machines misfeed my documents while churning out barely readable pages. Efax takes care of a lot of those problems. The company issues you a personal fax number—but when people send you a fax at that number, it appears as a graphic file attached to an e-mail. If you can't read it easily, you can magnify it before printing it. Efax also lets you send an e-mail to someone else's fax machine.
  - *Laserfiche* <www.laserfiche.com>. Document imaging systems especially for financial planners.

# CHAPTER 4

## Speaker Bureaus

These can be something of a catch-22. Many don't want to sign you until you have a track record as a speaker. But, once you get known as a speaker, as Ed Slott and others have shown, your speaking career may take on a life of its own. You may find that you no longer need a bureau that will take a slice of your fees.

Still, if you've gotten started, they may find new venues for you and help you expand your audience, and thus, your practice. And they may be able to help polish your presentation.

- *Executive Speakers Bureau <www.executivespeakers.com>*. This firm handles a lot of big-name speakers. Investing pioneer Muriel Siebert is on their list, as is Dee Hock, founder of VISA International.
- *Nationwide Speakers Bureau <www.nationwidespeakers.com>*. They represent some business and financial powerhouses, including Louis Rukeyser, Myron Kandel, and Abby Joseph Cohen.
- *Financial Forum <www.financialspeakers.com>*. This firm specializes in business and financial speakers. On their roster are Wharton's professor Jeremy Siegel, CNBC's Lawrence Kudlow, and economist Arthur Laffer.

## Speaker Resources

- *Toastmasters International <www.toastmasters.org>*. If you aren't comfortable speaking, try Toastmasters. Fees are very reasonable, and the organization boasts some 9,300 clubs worldwide, so there's probably one near you.

- *Local colleges.* Colleges and universities may also offer helpful courses. For example, New York University has an evening class titled "Speaking without Fear."

## Mailing Lists

- *DMG Direct* <www.dirmarketing.com>. A mailing list broker, DMG has access to 30,000 mailing lists. It says it can help even the smallest firms.
- *Dun & Bradstreet* <www.dnb.com>. Go here for mailing lists and a wide variety of other marketing resources.

# CHAPTER 5

## Professional Employer Organizations

These represent a wide range of companies that provide many different kinds of HR outsourcing services.

- *NetPEO* <www.netpeo.com>. This consulting and outsourcing company offers in-house and phone-based HR advice. It promises to help you with insurance plans, retirement plans, regulatory issues, recruiting, and payroll, among other services.
- *StaffMarket.com* <www.staffmarket.com>. This is actually not a professional employer organization (PEO) itself but more of a clearing center, which can put you in touch with a PEO that works in your area and handles your kind of business. Its services are free to businesses—it gets its fees from the member PEOs in its network.
- *The National Association of Professional Employer Organizations (NAPEO)* <www.napeo.org>. The professional organization of the PEO industry, it has about 400 members,

which are listed on the site by state. It also has a list of associate members who provide specific HR services. You can also read a description of PEOs and how they can help you.

- *Department of Labor (DOL)* <*www.dol.gov*>. There's a lot of information here for the smaller employer. The DOL provides a special section on small business regulatory compliance. The "Employment Law Guide" is well organized and covers many topics. Go to the DOL to learn your responsibilities under the Family and Medical Leave Act, for example, or the Americans with Disabilities Act.

# CHAPTER 6

## Newsletter and Brochure Outsourcing

These companies are in the business of providing newsletters and other publications for you to send to your clients. Some professional membership organizations do this for their members at minimal cost.

- *AdvisorProducts* <*www.advisorproducts.com*>. One of the leading companies in Web design also creates newsletters (see above).
- *Liberty Publishing* <*www.libertyink.com*>. With its own designers and editors, it creates personalized newsletters with compliant content appropriate for your clientele. Liberty has a range of publishing and mailing services and boasts some testimonials from top people in the financial business.
- *Newkirk* <*www.npi-opus.com*>. Offers the "Client Line" newsletter, which covers a variety of accounting, tax, and financial issues for your clients. Another product, its "Four Bits" newsletter, contains articles on estate planning, retire-

ment planning, saving and investing, and tax strategies. It has been cleared by the NASD.

## Web and Print Design Programs

- *Adobe Acrobat <www.adobe.com>.* A perfect tool for designing complex documents (see above).
- FrontPage <www.microsoft.com>. There are probably hundreds of programs that you can use to design your own Web page, if you are hell-bent on doing it yourself. Microsoft's FrontPage strikes a nice balance with both easy-to-use features for the relative novice and some sophisticated bells and whistles for the advanced user. Be patient—it takes more than an hour or two to get going with this.
- Publisher <www.microsoft.com>. Like its cousin, FrontPage, this is another Microsoft program that isn't too hard to learn to use yet has some advanced features. Again, don't expect to produce your own magazine after just a few minutes of playing with it.
- Go Daddy <www.godaddy.com>. This somewhat offbeat company, owned by Internet pioneer Bob Parsons, has some imaginative products and services to get you going on the Web quickly and simply—and at low cost. Check out the company's WebSite Complete Product.
- Quark Express <www.quark.com>. This is the gold standard of design programs. Top professional designers use this in leading national magazines. I'm only listing it here because there's a good chance you've heard of it and are thinking about getting it. Unless you have a trained, dedicated employee who can handle such a complex and sophisticated program, resist the urge.

# CHAPTER 8

## Professional Organizations

Following are some of the major national organizations. Many of them have state and regional chapters as well.

- *Financial Planning Association (FPA)* *<www.fpanet.org>*. You can get CFP CE through its magazine, the *Journal of Financial Planning*. Its annual Success Forum is one of the largest, most important planning conferences of the year. Local chapters also provide conferences with CE.
- *National Association of Insurance Financial Advisors (NAIFA)* *<www.naifa.org>*. This group of insurance-oriented planners has an annual conference with helpful sessions.
- *National Association of Personal Financial Advisors (NAPFA)* *<www.napfa.org>*. Even if you are not eligible to join this fee-only group, it offers many excellent sessions and networking opportunities at its annual spring conference and its four regional conferences.
- *American Institute of CPAs (AICPA)* *<www.aicpa.org>*. If it's convenient, the AICPA's personal financial planning conferences are useful even for non–CPAs.
- *Association for Investment Management and Research (AIMR)* *<www.aimr.org>*. AIMR's conferences tend to be very technical. They have some top speakers on high-end investing topics.
- *Investment Management Consultants Association (IMCA)* *<www.imca.org>*. IMCA offers some very good, investment-oriented events.

## Newsletters and Magazines

Most organizations have their own magazines and newsletters. Here are some unaffiliated publications. (In the interest of full disclosure, please note that I am the executive editor of *Financial Planning Magazine* and its associated Web site, Financial-Planning .com. In the interest of fairness, I am listing my publication's competitors as well.)

- Financial Planning *<www.financial-planning.com>*. Monthly magazine.
- Financial Advisor *<www.financialadvisormagazine.com>*. Monthly magazine.
- Investor Advisor *<www.ia-mag.com>*. Monthly magazine.
- Bloomberg Wealth Manager *<wealth.bloomberg.com>*. Monthly magazine.
- Investment News *<www.investmentnews.com>*. Weekly tabloid.
- Inc. Magazine *<www.inc.com>*. Not a financial planning publication like the others above, but it is particularly useful in running a business. Check out the Web site for specialized newsletters and other helpful info.

## Credentials

I'm going to get some nasty letters about the designations that I'm not listing here. The number of obscure designations seems to grow daily. There are too many out there to list, so I'm just listing some of the major ones and some places to get more information. The major groups tend to have standards for education and behavior.

- *Certified Financial Planner (CFP).* CFP Board of Standards <www.cfp.net>.

- *Chartered Financial Consultant (CFC) and Chartered Life Underwriter (CLU)*. The American College <www.amercoll.edu>.
- *Certified Public Accountant/Personal Financial Specialist. (CPA/PFS)*. American Institute of CPAs <www.aicpa.org>.
- *Certified Investment Management Analyst (CIMA)*. Investment Management Consultants Association <www.imca.org>.
- *Chartered Financial Analyst (CFA)*. The Association for Investment Management and Research <www.aimr.org>.
- *Certified Divorce Planner (CDP)*. The Institute for Certified Divorce Planners <www.institutecdp.com>.
- *Certified Fund Specialist (CFS)*. The Institute of Business and Finance <www.icfs.com>.
- *Registered Financial Consultant (RFC)*. The International Association of Registered Financial Consultants <www.iarfc.org>.

## Compliance Assistance

- *National Regulatory Services <www.nrs-inc.gov>*. This firm is the king of the compliance firms—they offer just about every kind of help you might want and are popular with many top advisors. (Another full disclosure note: they're owned by the same company that owns the magazine I work for.)
- *Blue Sky MLS <www.blueskymls.com>*. They offer a variety of outsourcing services for broker-dealers and investment advisors.
- *Vestment <www.vestment.net>*. Katherine Vessenes and Peter Vessenes are two of the profession's leading experts, and they provide a number of products and services related to practice management and compliance.
- *LiftBurden (the Consortium) <www.liftburden.com>*. Nancy Lininger offers consulting on compliance and other topics. She has no peer in explaining many complex technical topics simply.

## Miscellaneous

- *Bob Veres <www.bobveres.com>.* I wasn't sure where to mention him, but here is as good a place as any. Veres is a journalist who has been following this profession for as long as anyone can remember. His insights and opinions are invaluable. You can subscribe to his various newsletters on his site. His book, *The Cutting Edge in Financial Services,* is thought-provoking and mandatory reading for beginning professionals.

# Share the message!

### Bulk discounts
Discounts start at only 10 copies. Save up to 55% off retail price.

### Custom publishing
Private label a cover with your organization's name and logo. Or, tailor information to your needs with a custom pamphlet that highlights specific chapters.

### Ancillaries
Workshop outlines, videos, and other products are available on select titles.

### Dynamic speakers
Engaging authors are available to share their expertise and insight at your event.

Call Dearborn Trade Special Sales at 1-800-245-BOOK (2665)
or e-mail trade@dearborn.com

Dearborn™
Trade Publishing
A **Kaplan Professional** Company